W9-CKI-273

WORKING WITH DISADVANTAGED PARENTS AND THEIR CHILDREN

Working with Disadvantaged Parents and Their Children

SCIENTIFIC AND PRACTICE ISSUES

Sally Provence
Audrey Naylor

FOREWORD BY ALBERT J. SOLNIT

YALE UNIVERSITY PRESS
NEW HAVEN AND LONDON

Copyright © 1983 by Yale University.
All rights reserved.
This book may not be reproduced, in whole
or in part, in any form (beyond that
copying permitted by Sections 107 and 108
of the U.S. Copyright Law and except by
reviewers for the public press), without
written permission from the publishers.

Designed by Sally Harris
and set in Monticello type.
Printed in the United States of America by
Halliday Lithograph, West Hanover Mass.

Library of Congress Cataloging in Publication Data

Provence, Sally, 1916–
Working with disadvantaged parents and their children.
Bibliography: p.
Includes index.
1. Socially handicapped children—Service for
—United States—Longitudinal studies. 2. Socially
handicapped children—United States—Longitudinal
studies. 3. Family social work—United States—
Longitudinal studies. I. Naylor, Audrey, 1912–
II. Title.
HV741. P77 1983   362.8'2   82–48906
ISBN 0–300–02854–7

2   4   6   8   10   9   7   5   3   1

Contents

Foreword

BY ALBERT J. SOLNIT

. . . the past that breaks out in our hearts—Rilke

In this remarkable book, the authors describe infants who are at high risk of becoming damaged by their life's experience and demonstrate how to provide assistance for them and their parents that will help to overcome this risk. It should be emphasized that in the program described here this assistance was provided as services that the parents wanted for themselves and their children.

All human beings, children and adults, seek to know themselves as worthwhile and to feel that they are in charge of themselves. A crucial aspect of this sense of free will is to know one's history and not feel dominated or destroyed by it. As the only creatures capable of knowing their past, the story of their lives, human beings use constructions and reconstructions of the past to cope with their present and to anticipate and influence their future. The silent assumption of this longitudinal study is that each child is entitled to a useful and self-respecting past, one that gives him or her a sound sense of self-worth and of a future worth anticipating.

High-risk environments such as those associated with teenage pregnancy, poverty, disrupted families, single-parent families, and families with chronic illness promise a troubled, disrupted, depriving, traumatic past. By carefully describing and evaluating clinical service-oriented intervention research designed to transform high- into normative-risk environments, this book moves our theory and our practices significantly forward, demonstrating how to apply the force of our best knowledge in the service of enhancing each child's sense of his or her own history and self-worth. Such a history is associated with a progressive development in which the child's strengths can be elaborated and his weaknesses minimized or transformed into useful personal resources.

This is the second volume by these authors reporting on what has been demonstrated and learned in their service-centered research about the preventive and relieving aspects of clinical and educational services for infants born into high-risk environments and their parents. A high-risk environment is one which tends to complicate rather than facilitate a healthy development; it is one that uncovers and magnifies the infant's and parents' vulnerabilities rather than providing the built-in support that will enable them to overcome weaknesses or deficits. Thus, this book, along with its companion, *The Challenge of Daycare*, describes and demonstrates how to transform high-risk environments into environments in which the average expectable outcome is progressive development for the baby and the achievement of competence and self-fulfillment for the parents.

Both volumes carefully lay out the setting in which the services were offered and the guiding principles that shaped the interventions. The value of this study goes beyond this one project because such a model can be replicated in different settings throughout the United States and elsewhere with appropriate adaptation to the community and the high-risk environments of that locale.

As these books clearly indicate, it would be an error to equate high-risk environment only with poverty, though poverty is a major medium in which many high-risk environments are cultured. There are many other human situations and conditions with which high risk for infants and their parents can be associated. And the consequences are frequently transmitted from one generation to the next. The authors emphasize that effective intervention services can be provided in high-risk environments by competent multidisciplinary professionals and paraprofessionals who have learned to work together on a sustained basis. Such groups achieve effectiveness through their shared commitment, through resolving their intragroup tensions and conflicts and through the improvement they achieve from practicing together to provide services that are wanted by parents for their children and themselves.

It should not be necessary to learn anew that services must be sustained in order to reach the effectiveness that this program achieved; yet policy makers are always hoping to find some intervention which will serve as an inexpensive, one-shot "immunizing" agent. Most services cannot and do not work like polio vaccine. The clarification, support, and guidance provided by this program's health, educational, and social services are more analogous to the nurture that babies need on a daily basis to maintain their growth. Just as daily nurture should be sustained, these services should be supported long enough to enable parents in high-risk environments to love and care for their babies with increasing independence and satisfaction.

In this sense, our political rhythms, our preoccupation with short-cuts and economies, and our relative inability to plan for the long-term future tend to discourage or interfere with the sustained provision of attractive, accessible services for infants and their parents. After all, the impact of such services can seldom be sufficiently detected or measured in a few months. It is as though, despite understanding that the prevention and correction of malnutrition and the maintenance of normal growth require an adequate and balanced daily diet of calories, vitamins, minerals, proteins, carbohydrates, and fats over time, we persist in behaving as though a good meal now and then or a daily supplemental vitamin will suffice. Sustained, adequate daily nurture is needed throughout childhood. By finding ways of tapping and supporting the daily hopeful expectations and stimulation of loving, competent parents which infants need, this program successfully assisted parents in coping with high-risk situations.

Depending on the degree of risk in the human environment, such programs are affordable, though they are often viewed as being "too expensive." The cost of *not* having such programs is unbearable economically, socially, and in terms of the wasted lives of children who without these services are likely to become the dependent, sick, and unproductive adults of the future. Such children are also likely as parents to become the transmitters to the next generation of the deprivation, disorganization, and disruption that characterize those high-risk environments in which social deviation, educational deficits, and physical and mental ill health are evoked and elaborated. The exchange of long-term waste for short-term savings is tragic and economically malignant.

This book documents the reasons disadvantaged families should not have discontinuous services—i.e., no "poor services for poor people." The authors enable us to understand and share their deep conviction that children, especially young ones, cannot wait when they are in need of the basic care and services that are essential for healthy development. They describe how their team formed firm and productive voluntary alliances with disadvantaged parents in bringing about what all parents want: children who can grow up strong and competent, with a sense of pride in themselves, their families, and their community, able to become active agents in coping with and preparing to influence their environment so that it will be a sound one for for their own children in the next generation. As one parent said when her child was entering high school, "That program made a difference for my daughter and for me and the rest of the family. It was friendly, and it was what we needed."

This volume makes theoretical as well as practical contributions to our knowledge of how children develop, cope, and grow up in difficult or disadvantaged environments. In the bedrock of the parent-infant relationship, the personalities of the child and the parents unfold to their own interacting rhythms and needs. The authors show how the child extracts from these mutual experiences the identifications with the parents that lead to powerful continuities of attitudes and relationships as each child becomes his or her own person. Clearly, the services were designed to support parents in becoming autonomous, in becoming competent and proud of their children, and in strengthening the integrity of their family.

It is the hallmark of these authors to interweave practical know-how with theoretical sophistication. Their model serves practitioners and theoreticians equally well in gently reminding them how much we need to collaborate in bringing research and practice closer to each other. When theory informs practice and practice refines and elaborates theory, we are able, as the authors have demonstrated, to forge a strong chain of powerful assumptions and useful practices. Empirical observational and clinical data are linked to theoretical propositions that have continuing explanatory value. Thus, theory and its applications enrich ethically sound patterns of clinical practice.

In this research, the theoretical frame of reference is largely psychoanalytic; however, psychoanalytic theory has been adapted and
refined for practical application. The theory acts in the service of
explanation and, in the tradition of the natural sciences, is derived
from the empirical data. Thus, as in any well-working model, assessment of the impact of the services has resulted in revisions and
elaborations of psychoanalytic theory as well as raising questions
that can be viewed as theory-building constructs.

For example, as a result of this program and its assessment, it is
entirely clear that the psychoanalytic theory of object relations and
object constancy should be elaborated and revised. Future investigations should take into account how the mother can be supported
by others in fostering the mutual attachment of parent and infant
while assuring the primacy of their relationship, enabling the infant
to recognize the specificity of the parent and to differentiate the mother
from the non-mother. At the same time, the painstaking description
of how infant and parent perceive and respond to each other raises
fascinating and researchable questions about how the infant devel-
ops object constancy when there are two or more primary love objects—for example, when mother, father, grandmother, and maternal
aunt share the care of the baby. Does the baby know his or her mother
with specificity because she spends more time or is more influential
in the caretaking experiences? The authors have provided accounts
of nature and nurture interacting that will stimulate the reader to
think of such questions and many others at the cutting edge of our
quest for knowledge about young children.

The authors also make explicit how they weigh and interpret the
unavoidable contamination in service-centered clinical research when
the observer is also an active participant. This factor is further taken
into account in systematic follow-up studies that are highly respectful of the multitude of intervening variables. Throughout, the researchers struggle successfully to maintain a balance of focus and
openness.

Such research retains an awareness of the complexity of the observational field while prudently using theory to guide where and when
to observe, to intervene, and to make comparisons. In this way, lon-

gitudinal service-centered research seeks to retain a carefully defined focus with an openness to the large number of variables involved and to the need for useful comparisons. The researchers, practitioners and objective observers, have also been aware of the study's methodological limits because of the small sample and because the comparisons cannot be as rigorously controlled as in an experimental or "wet" laboratory investigation.

Valid data have been assured to the degree that the theory is useful in pointing to where and when to observe and in suggesting the range and hierarchy of interventions—for example, at times of normative developmental crises, such as weaning or separation. Reliability is assured to the degree that the observers are from several disciplines and that there is a balance of participant and nonparticipant observers who have worked well together under inspiring and inspired leadership. Significant data gathered by both participant and nonparticipant observers can be compared repeatedly and used to approximate and, whenever possible, to meet reliability standards.

Finally, this book extends our capacity to carry out service-centered studies: clinical research that is valid, humane, and ethical. The authors have shown that such research takes place in the context of abiding clinical alliances between researchers and subjects. Both research and services can lead to improved data collection, to a crucial sense of mutual respect and admiration between those doing the research and those being investigated and served, and to a reduction of the fear that disadvantaged people will be exploited by clinical investigators. Thus, there is a convergence of humanitarian values and better understanding when service-centered research is properly executed, with due respect for the conditions that make the research possible—informed consent, protection of confidentiality and privacy, and the assurance that these or other services sought by the parents will be available even if a parent should decide to discontinue participation in the research.

Acknowledgments

The project reported herein was supported by a grant from the United States Children's Bureau, Office of Child Development, Department of Health, Education, and Welfare, and we acknowledge with gratitude the encouragement and assistance of Charles Gershenson of the Office of Child Development. We are indebted to two directors of the Yale Child Study Center, Milton J. E. Senn and Albert J. Solnit, for their wisdom and encouragement as well as their tangible supports during the years of the study.

Members of the project staff deserve recognition for their contributions to the data as well as for their expert, devoted service to the children and parents. Some were with us throughout the five-year period, others for a shorter time. The pediatricians and developmental examiners involved in the project were Martha Leonard, Pamela (McKenzie) McBogg, and Gail Landy; the social workers were Catherine Cox, Mary Northup Christ, Marian Gray, Shirley Kirschner, and Jane Stockton; the nurses were Shirley Comer, Virginia McClellen, and Julina Rhymes Parker. Mary V. Kuhn, clinical psychologist, functioned as a developmental examiner and in the social work role with some of the families. Teachers and child-care staff were Elizabeth Owens, Susan Martin, Kirsten Dahl, Mildred Booker, Martha Dye, Karen Baldwin, Karen McKiver, and Margaret Frank. Alice Colonna contributed many hours as an expert observer. Arlene Richter's meticulous organization of schedules and records and her creative assistance at every stage is gratefully recognized, as is the secretarial work of Velma Inabinet, Betty Lubov, and Regina Pickus. Betty Clabby's typing of the manuscript as well as her work during the study were enormously helpful. The contributions of Demetra Parthenios, the project director's secretary, have been substantial, her steadiness and dedication exemplary.

Drs. Marianne Kris and Albert Solnit were particularly helpful as consultants on clinical material. Barbara Wolf Gerber and Leslie Rescorla brought their expertise as psychologists to the comparison and follow-up studies. Our colleagues in the Yale University Department of Psychology Edward Zigler, Penelope Trickett, Nancy Apfel, and Laurie Rosenbaum planned and carried out an independent follow-up study reported in Chapter 9. We thank them for their interest and research expertise and June Patterson for sophisticated educational consultation.

It has been a pleasure to work with Gladys Topkis, Maura Tantillo, Sally Serafim, and Sally Harris of the Yale University Press. We are grateful for their guidance and expertise. We acknowledge with thanks the financial assistance of Irving B. Harris and the Pittway Corporation Charitable Foundation and of the Herman G. and Suzanne G. Fisher Foundation during the writing period.

Most of all we are indebted to the families who joined us in this program. The greatest tribute to their participation would be society's acceptance of the importance of making such services as these available to young families.

Sally Provence, Project Director
Audrey Naylor, Assistant Project Director

PART I THE STUDY

CHAPTER 1

The Study
and Its Goals

The Yale Child Welfare Research Program* carried out at the Child Study Center from 1967 to 1972 was one of a number of ambitious, comprehensive research and demonstration projects undertaken in the 1960s to help disadvantaged families. The Yale project had several major goals. The primary objective was to help disadvantaged young parents to support the development of their children and to improve the quality of family life. Another goal was to develop effective ways of working with families that would be useful to service providers in diverse settings. Still another was to collect data that would make a contribution to child-development theory. A service-centered investigation and clinical-developmental approach were chosen as methods best suited to these goals.

The primary objective addressed a problem of growing national concern in the 1960s, the waste of human potential associated with poverty and with inadequate care of children in the early years. The project was planned with the expectation that if good services could be provided, disadvantaged young parents could be helped to rear their children in ways that would promote their development, allowing them to use their native endowment fully. We anticipated that services could be designed to reduce the risk factors for both parents and children associated with the poverty that denies them many of the resources available to others. We also anticipated that parents would need help to reduce as much as possible the stresses on themselves, both internal and external, that diminish their capacity to cope and adapt.

* Project no. PR900 of the United States Children's Bureau, Office of Child Development, Department of Health, Education, and Welfare.

An intensive program for a small number of families, the project was housed in a remodeled old residence, Children's House, in New Haven's inner city. It began with a pilot project, or phase I, involving twenty-three children ages 14 months to 4 years. The pilot program was useful for trying out and refining methodology and gaining experience in using new methods and modifying traditional ones. Phase II was planned to begin during the first pregnancy of the participating mothers. The objectives and general design of both phases were virtually the same, and experience in both provided the data for *The Challenge of Daycare* (Provence, Naylor, and Patterson 1977). Only the seventeen families who joined the study during phase II are the subjects of the present report. The families were all members of the so-called culture of poverty, yet in their diversity they were also representative of children and parents of all socioeconomic groups.

We were influenced in our choice of both services and methods of study by the view that those closest to the child, his parents, exert the strongest influence on his development and that his development would be best followed, protected, and promoted by the study staff through a continuing and close association with his parents—a partnership in behalf of the child. We believed that this would come about through offering those services needed by parents and children of all classes and races: medical care, education, and social and psychological services. We anticipated that such services would provide not only the specific help the parents sought but also an opportunity for a working relationship to form over time as parents developed trust in those who worked with them. The continuity of relationship between each parent and child and the investigators would, we expected, provide a rich and varied context for the study of the child, enhancing research data as well as increasing the scope and effectiveness of the services.

Clinical assessment of the functioning and needs of parent and child provided us with the basis for individualizing services. We used clinical methods and constructs in collecting, organizing, and evaluating research data. Our approach was that both parenthood and the child's physical, mental, social, and emotional growth could best be viewed as developmental processes. We also regarded the process through which a staff becomes an effective team as developmental.

A conviction that grew out of our clinical experience was that to be effective services must be individualized. Thus, an important factor in the effectiveness of the work would be to come to know insofar as possible the individual characteristics of each child and parent over time. We expected that the services needed by a specific child or parent at one time would differ from those needed earlier or later and from those needed by another family. The effectiveness of the services, we believed, would depend not only on their availability and their quality but also on how well they fit the current needs of the families; therefore it would be influenced by our sensitivity to those needs. In coming to know the parents, we sought to assess their psychological readiness to use, for example, suggestions, advice, intercession with a community agency, or a psychodynamic interpretation. In looking at the child, we had to take into account the rapidly changing characteristics that are reflections of the developmental process along with individual traits. In anticipating the outcome of our program we were guided by previous experience in clinical and educational work with families of various socioeconomic and racial groups that led us to appreciate the wide individual differences within supposedly homogeneous populations. Thus the ability to be flexible within the framework of services of good quality— flexible about their timing and the way they were presented and carried out—would, we expected, be an important determinant of the effectiveness of the services, and flexibility was adopted as a guiding principle of the program.

In addition to the information gained through interviews and physical and developmental testing, we expected that direct observation of the behavior of a child and parents would contribute data essential to the research and service goals. Systematic observation of behavior in varying environments, from those considered normal to many atypical situations, is a well-established method of study. Developmental and clinical theories have been enriched through using this approach. Granted the limitations of understanding the young child's psychological life from surface behavior, observation is an important window into the child's mind. (Freud and Burlingham 1944; Spitz 1945, 1950; Hartmann 1950; Kris 1950, 1975; Kessen 1965.)

In its study aspect, the program was developed as a type of action research in which the investigator not only observes but *acts* within the field of observation and is part of the process being studied. The investigator's awareness of the influence he exercises is an important part of the data. Bias and distortion of recall were guarded against by using some staff members as observers of many contacts with the families but without direct involvement with them. These investigators were also familiar with data resulting from the service providers' work. In staff conferences, the contributions of these investigators served to supplement and at times to modify the impressions of those directly involved with each family—pediatrician, social worker, psychologist, and teacher.

In addition to our own earlier research and clinical experience and that of others, developmental theory, especially constructs from psychoanalytic child psychology, had an important influence on the project. These constructs are spelled out and their specific applicability to the project described in Chapter 3. We were particularly influenced by propositions regarding the role of parent-child relationships in the child's emotional and cognitive development. The biological dimensions of our approach include developmental processes encompassing such key concepts as endowment, maturation, phase specificity, and adaptation. The project was also shaped by an awareness of the importance of the societal subsystems which influence children and their parents.

We recognized full well the limitations of any particular research method or strategy. Especially in the complex field of human behavior, any plan of study supplies only partial answers; any observational technique makes visible only part of the total field. We hoped that as a result of the study some issues would be clarified and plausible answers to a few questions about methods of intervention would be provided. In addition, we expected to generate new hypotheses that might be pursued through further investigation.

The next chapter describes the study population, the staff, and the program's services and is followed by a chapter on the theoretical approach. In chapters 4, 5, 6, 7, and 8 the major focus is on how the work was done, with representative cases presented in detail. Chapter 9 reports the results of intervention at the end of the project and five years after its close. The results as described by Rescorla, Provence, and Naylor (1982) and by Trickett, Apfel, Rosenbaum, and Zigler (1982) in an independent study are included in part. Chapter 10 provides a retrospective evaluation of the usefulness of the conceptual framework and the effectiveness of the practice. It attempts further to understand the outcome of the study and to suggest the study's implications for organizing and delivering effective services for other disadvantaged children and their parents—that is, to identify what can be generalized.

CHAPTER 2

The Study Population, Staff, and Services

Study Population

The subjects of the study were seventeen low-income families with a total of eighteen children* who participated in the project from the child's birth to 30 months of age. We identified young pregnant women attending the obstetrical clinic of the Yale–New Haven Medical Center who met the following criteria: they were primiparas who resided in the inner city, with incomes at or below the federal poverty guidelines, who were not markedly retarded or actively psychotic and had no serious complications of pregnancy. Twenty-five women who fit these criteria were interviewed; twenty agreed to participate. Of these twenty families, one family withdrew from the project, one child was stillborn, and one child was born with a biological handicap. The handicapped child and his parents were given full services, but are not included in this report.

During the preliminary meeting with each mother the project was explained and a descriptive brochure was presented which provided the same information given by the interviewer: that the purpose of the study was to help parents promote the development of their child and to help the family through providing access to medical care for the child, daycare or nursery school, and social services. The parent's obligations in joining the study were to be willing to come to Children's House at regular intervals for the child's physical and developmental examinations and to be available for interviews approximately every other week at home and at Children's House. At a

---

* A second child of one of the families was included in the study.

second interview, which if possible included the prospective father, the services and obligations were discussed in greater detail. In the intake process we emphasized the importance of the parents' role in helping their child develop and on the mutuality of the work to be done. We saw parents as many times as necessary to answer fully any questions they had about the project and to give them an opportunity to appraise us, as we were appraising them, before a mutual decision about their joining the study was reached. The care taken with the admission process was very likely an important factor in maintaining the continuity of the study. Even more important was the continuity provided by a stable staff. One family dropped out fairly early, after the only instance of our having to change both the pediatrician and the social worker with whom they had started.

Of the eighteen children, twelve were black, two were white, two were Puerto Rican, one had a white mother and a black father, and one had a white mother and a father of black and Puerto Rican parentage. There were eleven boys and seven girls. Six of the mothers were married, five in conventional marriages and one in a common-law marriage. Two others were married but separated, with divorces pending. Nine were single. At the point of admission the six two-parent families were self-supporting; the two mothers who were separated from their husbands were on public welfare, as were seven of the single women. Of the other two single women, one was supported by her parents and the other had been self-supporting and was so again after the birth of her baby. The age range of the mothers was 18 to 24 years.* Their backgrounds varied: About a third had moved from the rural South during adolescence, coming from large, poor, usually two-parent families. Another third came from poor inner-city families in the Northeast. The remaining third included one woman from Puerto Rico, one who came from a very disorganized family of children of different fathers, and several from intact working-class families with emotional disturbances. Eleven mothers and eight fathers had finished high school. Many of them felt that the quality of their education had been poor.

---

* The project did not include younger adolescents because at the time there was a service-centered study of young mothers in progress in the medical center.

The study population was unfortunately reduced by the unavailability of all but six fathers for involvement in the project. Either directly or through the mothers the fathers living in the area were urged to participate. Eleven did not. In two instances the married couples were separated; in nine others the parents had never married. Of these, three fathers were married to other women, two had broken off with the mother when the pregnancy was discovered, two had only occasional contact with the mother after pregnancy, and two had left the community. None of the eleven nonparticipating fathers assumed a consistent parental role with the study child, though some occasionally gave gifts or small contributions of money. Of the six fathers who agreed to participate, we worked intensively with two and had varying degrees of contact with the other four. The fact that several had to work at two jobs in order to support their families meant that their participation was minimal. Because it was not possible to develop data about the fathers comparable to those about the mothers and children, the focus in what follows is almost exclusively on the mothers and children.

The Staff and Services

We began with a staff made up of both well-qualified professionals and promising paraprofessionals. It was organized into four major work groups or units: (1) pediatrics: responsible for the medical care of the children; (2) developmental appraisal: physicians and psychologists responsible for periodic assessment of each child's development; (3) teaching, nursing, and child care: responsible for a program of child care and education regarded as a unified function; (4) social work: responsible for working with parents and for liaison with other staff. A team made up of one person from each of the four areas of responsibility was assigned to each family. The family teams provided coordinated services. They also recorded work with and observations of the families to which they were assigned. There were other staff members who observed regular pediatric and developmental examinations and child care and education but had no direct contact with the families. Observations by both the participant and the nonparticipant observers contributed to our knowledge of the families for research purposes and were of immediate usefulness in efforts to help families lessen or resolve problems.

Pediatrics

Pediatricians first met the mothers (and some fathers) shortly before delivery and were responsible for medical care of the children from birth on. The antepartum interview was oriented primarily toward acquainting parents with the pediatrician, explaining the service, and answering any questions the prospective parents might have. Maternal preference regarding rooming-in versus regular nursery, breast feeding versus bottle feeding, and general plans about the help mothers would have at home during the first weeks were discussed.

The child's pediatrician, who was present at the delivery whenever possible, saw the newborn and mother at least once a day and sometimes more often during the two to four days of the lying-in period. Scheduled observations of the newborns included a standard medical examination and neonatal behavioral observations, the latter resembling the Brazelton Scale (1973), which was not then available. Pediatricians scheduled home visits within the first week and initiated weekly contact by telephone thereafter for the first month. Infants were brought to the clinical rooms at Children's House for their first office visit at one month of age. Routine visits to the center were scheduled monthly for the first twelve months and thereafter at three-month intervals. All pediatric examinations at the center were observed by other members of the research staff as well.

The rationale for having the doctor take the initiative in making contact related to the almost universal need of young parents for support in caring for their child during the early months of their experience as parents. The experience of many pediatric practitioners is that their ready availability during the early weeks to answer questions, listen to parental concerns, and give appropriate recommendations for care reduces maternal anxiety and enables mothers to become selective about the use of medical care more quickly than if during this time the doctor responds only to crises. Another determinant of this policy was our expectation that this group of parents might be hesitant to call the doctor unless actively encouraged to do so. For each family there was one main pediatrician; a back-up pediatrician also became well known to them. This reflected another strong conviction of the project staff: *that continuity of health care of the children by a primary physician would be of central importance in helping parents to provide good child care, in building their confidence in themselves as parents, and in enabling them to utilize the services provided by the project to the fullest extent they could.* House calls were made as needed. After the first weeks, these were usually but not always calls to see children who were ill. The parents' knowledge that the doctor was available when needed was no small part of their attachment to the project. The pediatricians' capacity to respond promptly and with specificity was greatly enhanced by their coming to know the parents and children individually and well.

The protection of the health of the child in a comprehensive sense was as much a part of the pediatricians' role as the treatment of illness. In their relationship with parents there was emphasis from the beginning on helping parents voice their questions and observations about their children and on helping them to feel increasingly confident of their own ability to decide when they needed to see or talk with the doctor. Respectful listening, helping to clarify questions or concerns, and inviting parents' opinions were some of the ways in which they encouraged parents to participate actively in the health care of their children. To facilitate this process, up to an hour was allotted for periodic examinations. Both the information and the psychological support provided were seen as important. Pediatricians gave advice about child rearing as well as about illness, not in recipe form but in specific relation to individual children and parents. Because the project pediatricians were also child-development specialists their records were rich in developmental and behavioral as well as health data.

The pediatricians' records as research data were of several types, most of which conformed to a preplanned outline: the antepartum interview, neonatal pediatric exam, neonatal behavioral observations, and the monthly well-baby examination. Growth and immunization records were kept on standard forms. House calls, phone calls, and other illness records were simply dictated as narratives. Observations by the social worker and a nonparticipant observer of the child, the parent, and the pediatrician during the pediatric examinations completed the pediatric data that became part of each family record. A copy of the outline for recording the regular health examination is included in Appendix 3 because the standard form has been augmented.

Developmental Appraisal

Developmental examinations, using the Yale Developmental Schedules, were administered to the children at 2, 3, 6, 9, 12, 18, 24, and 30 months of age by examiners who were not providing other services for the children they tested. Developmental evaluations took place in conjunction with but preceding regular pediatric examinations, in the presence of one or both parents. The results were passed on to parents by the tester or social worker or pediatrician, each of whom contributed to further discussion as needed. One benefit of these sessions was that parents became interested in specific characteristics of their children such as their way of solving problems, their interests, and often their sensitivities. The fact that the examiner became a familiar person facilitated the sharing of observations and information. We were to learn in the follow-up interviews of another benefit derived in part from parent participation in the developmental examinations: They helped parents to view development as a process that could be influenced by the child's daily experiences both in the center program and at home.

The test sessions took place in a room with a one-way mirror, with furniture appropriate to the age of the child—for example, crib and tabletop for infants not yet sitting alone, high chair and tabletop for toddlers, low table and chair for those aged 2 years and above. A cabinet contained the test material and toys. Chairs for parents and examiner completed the setup. The room contained a foldaway table that was used during the pediatric examination.

It was part of the plan to make the child and parent as comfortable

as possible during the testing; that is, we did not intend to introduce
contrived stresses of any kind. The test situation itself, we reasoned,
with its increasing task orientation over time, would introduce variable stresses for child and parent. The child's test performances and
the parent's behavior would be influenced not only by the child's
developmental status but also by fatigue, illness and other discom-
forts, physical and psychological, by the current relationship of each
child and parent, and by their reactions to the examiner. Two of the
research staff observed each developmental examination, as they did
the pediatric examination. One made a narrative recording of child-
parent-examiner interactions. The other recorded details of the infant's behavior and test performance. The examiner was responsible
for observations as well as for scoring the test and dictating a summary. To collect quantifiable developmental data was, of course, one
aim. In addition, the behavior of the infant or toddler in the situation, including *how* he did what he did, was deemed important: the
energy and zest with which he approached the materials and tasks,
the ego's control over motility, problem solving, speech, and so forth;
the rapidity of regression under stress or resistance to it; the child's
way of relating to parent and examiner; his ways of reacting to and
coping with anxiety, physical pain, frustration, and so on. From these
records and other observations of the infant (at home, in daycare or
toddler school) we were able to construct profiles of the child's developing personality as well as to derive the profiles of development
according to the norms of the standardized test.

In terms of ego development the tests were especially useful for
recording the development of the autonomous functions of the ego.
Motility, speech, intelligence, memory, visual and auditory perception, the capacity for delay, and, to some extent, the organizing function could be followed with reasonable confidence. The development of the child's relationships with others was inferred partly from
the test situation also. Coping behavior, as Lois Murphy (1974) has
indicated, gives important clues about vulnerability and resilience in
the infant and toddler, and some of these behaviors were systemati-
cally observed in the test situation. At times the coping behaviors,
problem solving, and other reactions to challenge or stress permitted

us to make inferences that could be stated as tentative formulations about the development of mechanisms of defense. Thus, all of these areas of development were in part assessed from the observations of the test situation to which was added information from all other sources of data. Appendix 5 gives test reports on two of the children which illustrate the form of the test summary.

Daycare and Toddler School

Our program of child care and education was based on a view of how children develop and learn and on a commitment to plan in accordance with developmental needs. Some of the underlying developmental propositions which we translated into practice included (1) the phase concept, with emphasis on specific tasks, competencies, styles of interaction, typical conflicts, needs, and vulnerabilities; (2) the central role of human relationships and how these influence learning for better or worse; (3) the interdependence of cognitive, emotional, and social development. Derivatives and corollaries of these fundamental constructs provided the rationale behind the introduction of certain program elements at particular times, lying behind the handling of the separation experiences for parent and child, and helping to determine the staffing patterns planned in relation to the child's need for continuity of contact with a primary caregiver, and recognizing the individuality of each child. In full daycare, teaching had to be intimately concerned with providing for the child's bodily needs in addition to knowing his tempo, feelings, and style of learning, thus combining nurturing and teaching roles. In short, the educational approach was addressed to the whole child, and strong efforts were made to arrange experiences that would enhance his physical, intellectual, and emotional development.

The program of child care and education has been fully presented and illustrated in *The Challenge of Daycare* (Provence, Naylor, and Patterson 1977), where in Chapter 6 we discussed developmental needs under the headings of (1) physical care; (2) a supportive physical environment; (3) responsiveness to individual needs; (4) opportunities to act upon the environment; (5) an enriching affective atmosphere; (6) a speaking social partner; (7) consistency and repetition, variety and contrast; (8) toys and other playthings; (9) quiet moments; and (10) limits, prohibitions, and expectations for conformity. We defined what we had to do in order to meet these needs and presented descriptions of children, staff, the setting, and activities which illustrated our efforts to provide a nurturing and enriching environment in a daycare center. Differences in the program according to the children's ages, from infancy through the preschool years, were fully described. We will not repeat details of this aspect of the program here. Instead, we give some observations from the program in Appendix 1. One of the recording forms used for situational and developmental observations made in daycare and toddler school is in Appendix 4. From the observations made by both teacher-caregivers and observers, a few have been selected to exemplify what daycare of the very young involves, what infants and toddlers do at various ages, what the staff does. No attempt is made to illustrate all aspects of planning and carrying out the program.

Twelve of the study children were in the daycare program for varying lengths of time over the period of the study. Five had twenty or more months in daycare, five had from ten to nineteen months and two had five months or less. Some began as early as 6 weeks of age; others, not until well into the second year. For five children who did not need daycare, a toddler school was held twice a week for an hour and a half with their mothers present. Children began toddler school between 15 and 18 months of age and continued until they were 30 months. One child was in neither daycare nor toddler school.

The contacts with parents and children in the daycare and toddler school program provided important sources of information, contributing much to our knowledge of the families, to their knowledge of us, and to the working relationship. In the daycare setting parents had contact not only with the children's caregiver-teachers but with their social workers, pediatricians, and other members of the project staff: the cook, the handyman, the secretaries, the observers, the project director, and staff members who worked with other families. As the one setting in which it was natural for all staff and all families to come together, it contributed to a feeling of kinship and shared interest.

Parents usually became comfortable first with one of the caregivers and gradually with others. Their trust in the competence of the staff developed similarly. They were told on arrival that they were welcome to stay as long as they wished. At the end of the day, too, they were invited to linger. The informal atmosphere created by the staff in the comfortable old house helped parents feel at home. Sometimes parent and caregiver exchanged information about the child or about family events over a cup of coffee. As relationships developed, many matters besides those related to child care were discussed. For example, two mothers whose children entered daycare as very young infants used the older women who cared for their babies much as they might have used their own mothers, had they been available, asking advice about their own clothing or about where to buy something, or simply sharing events of their day, its frustrations or pleasures. Individual relationships, of course, varied. But there was always the intent in daycare and other situations to convey to parents our interest in hearing their wishes, opinions, and concerns about their children and to create an atmosphere, a social climate, in which such communication would be possible. In our staffing patterns and program planning we emphasized that continuity in the relationship between the young child and the caregiver was important in his learning and in his feeling of security in daycare. But of more vital importance, we believed, was the child's relationship with his parents, and it was our aim to support it in every way we could in all aspects of our work.

Social Work

The primary goal of the study—to promote the development of disadvantaged children—could not be achieved, we believed, without entering into a partnership with parents that recognized their crucial role in their child's development. Thus, we planned for direct intervention with parents. That was chiefly the responsibility of the social work component, which was staffed mainly by psychiatric social workers but also by a clinical psychologist and psychiatric nurse, each working with two families. The major goal of the social work component was to offer parents whatever psychological and social services were needed and could appropriately be supplied. It was our assumption that reducing stress from any source and increasing the parent's capacity to cope with it would benefit not only the parent but, indirectly, the child. A secondary but nonetheless important function was to provide a link between the home and the center. These responsibilities involved the following four tasks:

1. To learn what problems each parent faced. We needed to assess which stemmed from reality factors due to poverty and the consequent lack of the kind of resources available to others, which were the psychological consequences of years of second-class citizenship, and which were related to personality factors that might or might not be accessible to psychological intervention.

2. To give direct child-care advice when it was sought by parents or to help them to seek it when in our judgment it was needed. The frequent ineffectiveness of unsolicited advice, whether given by friends, relatives, or professionals, has long been recognized.

3. To provide a major part of the necessary liaison between the home and the center. Contact with social workers was not intended to substitute for contacts between parents and daycare or other staff. However, because parents had the most contact with the social workers, the latter coordinated the child's home and daycare experiences, dealt with special requests or complaints about the program, and supplied relevant information from the home situation when concern about a child prompted staff problem-solving efforts.

4. To serve as advocates for parents with community agencies when necessary and help parents to become their own advocates.

A sample of the recording form for social work activity is provided in Appendix 2.

As the pilot phase of the intervention program was getting under way in the late 1960s, many were questioning whether white middle-class professionals could work effectively with those in the culture of poverty, especially those of minority races. We thought they could. If tension over differences in race and culture existed in specific instances, we engaged parents in discussing the differences between us, especially the racial differences, and did not try to avoid or minimize them. There was, of course, variability in the effectiveness of the work with parents. However, in no case can our failure to achieve a particular goal with a parent be best understood as due to alienation based on racial, cultural, or socioeconomic differences. Because the services offered met people "where they lived," alliances were created that diminished the stress that might be evoked by differences in economic and ethnic background. It was and is our conviction that the respect one has for another person and the sensitive effort one makes to establish real communication are far more important in determining ability to work together than race and background.

Each parent—fathers included, when possible—had frequent, regular appointments with the social worker, who more than any other staff member was "the parents' person," identified more clearly in the short term with the parents' needs, interests, and goals than with the needs of the child. Some appointments by plan were in the home, allowing the social worker to learn about the home environment and to make observations of parent-child interaction there. There were also scheduled office interviews, many informal contacts in the center, and both formal and informal observations of parent-child interaction. Interviews were held at least biweekly the first year and thereafter as individual need indicated. Parents were encouraged to call upon their social worker whenever they wanted to.

Each social worker was an experienced and competent practitioner in the problem-centered situation of a mental health clinic for young children that served families representing most racial groups and all socioeconomic levels in the community. Nevertheless, we felt some trepidation about how transferable these skills would be to the new tasks. We recognized that this situation differed in one critical respect from that of the clinic. The initial focus on the concerns of parents which bring them to seek help in a clinic would not be supplied by the study parents, not at first and perhaps not later. Thus, some modification of traditional ways of working was necessary. However, we anticipated that a few basic concepts from clinical experience would be useful in beginning work with parents. They were these:

One must begin with empathic concern for the parent. Regardless of a parent's racial, cultural, and socioeconomic status, parenthood in addition to its satisfactions can be and often is a difficult stage of life even for one who ordinarily functions well. For those whose own nurturing was poor and whose life experience has been stressful, aptitude for parenting is often impaired in spite of their wish to be good parents. Parents who have not been adequately nurtured in their own growing-up years may need to be given to in certain ways before they can tolerate others giving to their child. Parents with better nurturing may still have trouble with child rearing because of unusual stresses in their everyday lives, or because the infant's rhythms and characteristics are discordant with their own. Help with parenting may not be effective if given via the direct route of advice about child care, whether solicited or not. Rather, better parenting may be possible mainly as an indirect result of helping the adult to reduce his own psychological neediness and stress. Parents are not just parents; they are adults, each with his or her own set of strengths and limitations. If one is to help them, there is no substitute for respecting each individual as the unique human being he or she is. There is no substitute for sensitive attention and response to both manifest and symbolic communication that allow the parent to feel that he or she has been heard. Such communication is essential to building a relationship in which the parent feels safe in sharing the information, concerns, thoughts, and feelings that can lead to problem solving, whether by increasing capacity to cope with stress or by changing maladaptive behavior.

These guiding principles served us well. The methods and skills of clinical practice that have been cited, as well as others, were highly applicable to our work. But we did modify practice, sometimes by plan and sometimes as intuitive responses. Because most parents did not know what to expect or how we might be able to help them and thus usually at first brought no agenda of their own to interviews, we had to be relatively active, to take more responsibility for the focus of interviews. We could not assume the more passive stance appropriate in psychotherapy. We had be careful, however, that in being active we did not become intrusive. The eagerness to know each parent well in order ultimately to be helpful had to be tempered by sensitivity to subtle, often nonverbal clues about what each individual was or was not ready to allow us to know. In situations of initial cultural gap between the interviewer and the parent, we found it was important not to let the interviewer become the object for fantasy and projection. Instead, to a judicious extent we volunteered relevant information about ourselves, sometimes drew on personal experiences, identified as such, when doing so was useful in communicating, and answered innocuous questions about ourselves.

A major difference from usual practice in, for example, a child guidance clinic was the possibility of offering parents help with various reality problems as well as psychological help. We tried, as stated, to lessen as much as possible whatever stresses each family was experiencing, partly through helping them to work toward whatever their own goals were for a better life. We found that it was possible in the context of a sound, professional relationship to provide both psychological help and various specific services. However, the relationship had to reach a stage of trust before parents felt secure enough to tell us what they hoped to achieve. We had to use clinical judgment to decide on the psychologically feasible time to offer tangible help. If offered prematurely or insensitively, it was either not used or misused. The kinds of assistance given were highly variable, but among the more usual were help in getting training, education, better jobs, better housing, birth control information, and medical care. Our objective was not only to help parents achieve their goals but also to increase their capacity to function effectively on their own behalf, to heighten their self-esteem, and to enable them to take more charge of their own lives. Important in this aspect of the work was conveying to parents, when appropriate, our belief in their potential for reaching the goals they had in mind.

Parents used interviews in a variety of ways. We tried always to be responsive to whatever concerns they expressed, no matter how indirectly or obscurely they expressed them. But when appropriate we also attempted to arouse or heighten their interest in the child's progress both in the center and at home. Some parents brought up problems they had with their child at home while others tended not to. Child-care advice was not ordinarily given gratuitously. However, when a child's problem was one that could not be resolved through our care of him at the center and was due to the parent's behavior with the child, we didn't hesitate to try to involve the parent in a fruitful discussion. Some parents could not engage in the kind of examination of their own feelings and motives that might have resulted in changing maladaptive behavior with their child and others important to them, but others could and did. Parents introduced some concerns directly, some indirectly. Concerns that could be brought up directly usually had to do with external rather than internal problems: for example, failure of the housing authority to provide an apartment free of lead-based paint or failure of the welfare department to replace a check stolen from the family mailbox. Problems presented by indirection were usually those involving strong feelings, often covered by a façade of initial blandness. The more productive interviews were usually the result of the interviewer's being able to involve the parent in exploring what lay beneath the concern as initially presented so that problem solving could begin.

The following are illustrations of the way in which problems were introduced and the underlying issues parents could be helped to address.

Mrs. A.—The manifest problem: a mild complaint but with anger close to the surface because her son had come home wearing freshly laundered socks that were not his own. The underlying issue: conflicted feelings about her white child being in a program with black children and still more conflicted feelings about herself being in a program with black parents.

Mrs. B.—The manifest problem: worry over her 18-month-old daughter's difficult, controlling behavior. The underlying issue:

Mrs. B.'s guilt over the daily separation from her child in day-care and consequent overindulgence of her at home. It was as if the child sensed her mother's guilt and exploited it. She was becoming a little tyrant, and her mother was feeling a failure.

Mr. and Mrs. C.—The manifest problem: anger at their son for his difficult behavior. The underlying issue: guilt over their loss of patience with a child who was overactive and irritable from birth coupled with a wish to learn how to respond to him more helpfully.

Mrs. D.—The manifest problem: concern that a facial grimace developed by her child following a viral infection would be permanent. The underlying issue: Mrs. D.'s belief that God was punishing her in this way because of an earlier failure to follow medical advice. The mother's view of her child as permanently damaged was being taken over by the child, who was beginning to act the part of a semi-invalid.

Mrs. E.—The manifest problem: fatigue because she wasn't getting enough sleep. The underlying issue: anger that her child's long naps in daycare were causing a nighttime sleep disturbance that was upsetting both parents. Just at this time we were concluding that long naps were part of the child's reaction to separation. The mother's fortuitous complaint allowed us to work on the separation with both parents and child, with the result that the parents got more sleep and the child began to use the program more profitably.

Mrs. F.—The manifest problem: the father's lack of interest in helping with family decisions. The underlying issue: the father's alcoholism. Exploration led to Mrs. F.'s wish to evaluate the marriage and resolve her indecision about whether or not to end it.

In some of these examples, lessening or resolving both manifest and underlying concerns of parents was of direct help to the children; in others, the help was indirect and related to stress reduction in the parent.

Interdependence of the Services

The unique contributions of each component of the service would have been of less value to the families if they had not been brought together as integrated parts of a whole. The members of each family team were in continuous contact with one another, sharing observations and information, and could make use of an ongoing synthesis of data from all sources as an aid in working out ways to help children and parents about whom concern developed. This integrative process, carried out in frequent formal and informal discussions of the entire project staff, helped in clarifying the goals of the project and the philosophy of how to work effectively with both children and parents over time. To quote from *The Challenge of Daycare*:

> As our experience and our data about both children and parents accumulated, and as patterns and trends began to emerge, our research goals prompted us to attempt theoretical formulations, to develop hypotheses, and to make predictions. This allowed us over time to test both the adequacy of our data and the validity of our formulations. Gradually, as we became concerned about particular children, our discussions took on more immediacy and urgency. Sometimes as we pooled our data and began to put together a picture of a child's functioning in the center, compiling information from episodic material, assessments prepared by the teacher, the results of developmental testing, descriptions of his functioning at home, and assessments of the current home environment, concern was aroused. After the first few months, comparisons with earlier assessments of each child allowed us to be aware of his progress or lack of it in various areas of development. [P. 33]

From these discussions, we arrived at decisions about the next step in the work with child and parent. The clinical model for this kind of procedure was, of course, the traditional case conference in which information from all sources is contributed and synthesized and recommendations are developed.

CHAPTER 3

Theoretical Concepts
and Clinical Perspectives

The variety, complexity, and interdependence of factors that influence the health and development of the young child and the expansion and alternatives that occur at every developmental stage make it challenging to present succinctly the conceptual basis for the intervention program. The danger is of oversimplifying propositions and of making direct and linear connections between, for example, certain child-rearing practices and certain characteristics of a child's development or adjustment. Such selective descriptions tempt one to see a specific phase or a specific measure of infant care or a specific illness or traumatic experience as the sole factor influencing developmental outcome. However, because we are interested in reporting to others a particular program of intervention with infants in a population considered at high risk for developmental difficulties, and because we did, indeed, consciously and intentionally utilize certain developmental and clinical constructs, it is necessary that we spell out the conceptual frame of reference as clearly as we can.

In this chapter we emphasize a number of clinically applicable theoretical and empirical concepts regarding health, development, and behavior, which provided the guidelines for clinical work with children and parents and for child care and education. As will be recognized, these concepts come mainly from clinical pediatrics and psychiatry, psychoanalysis and developmental psychology, clinical social work and early childhood education. For years preceding the intervention project, the clinical and educational practices derived from these theoretical and empirical approaches had been applied to the evaluation and treatment of developmental and mental-health problems of infants and young children in the Child Development

26

Unit of the Yale Child Study Center. The specific way of bringing the material together, of selecting and organizing the concepts, has been determined by their clinical usefulness tested over a period of years. The coherence is based on their heuristic relevance for understanding development and the guidelines they provide in the diagnosis and treatment of early childhood disorders. They are described under the following nine headings:

1. Endowment
2. Maturation and Development
3. Environment and Experience
4. The Phase or Stage Concept
5. Parenthood as a Developmental Process
6. The Central Role of Human Relationships
7. Physical Care of the Child
8. Play and the Young Child's Development
9. Learning, Coping, and Adaptation

Propositions from psychoanalytic developmental psychology are strongly represented in this set of constructs, especially those aspects of theory concerning the importance of human relationships in development and selected constructs from ego psychology regarding learning and adaptation.

Endowment

The child's endowment at birth is a function not only of genetics but also of the intra-uterine and neonatal environments and the events surrounding birth. Any biological defect or special vulnerability may interfere with development. Thus infants may be seriously challenged prenatally by poor nutrition, infection, toxicity, trauma, or other health problems of the pregnant woman; they may be born with skeletal defects, structural defects of the central nervous system, errors of metabolism, or other biochemical aberrations; neonates may suffer from respiratory distress, infection, or trauma. When the physiological processes or anatomical structures are impaired, future development may be jeopardized. Moreover, the development of biologically impaired infants is more likely to be impeded by adverse environmental conditions than is the development of normally endowed infants.

But normal infants, too, differ from one another at birth in ways that have been recognized and described. Though the nature and significance of these differences are not fully understood, there is evidence that they partially define the infant's individual patterns of development and contribute in substantial ways to the course of development and organization of behavior.

Differences in the reaction patterns of newborn babies have been observed. Many investigators—among them Peiper (1949); Fries and Woolf (1953); Richmond and Lustman (1955); Lustman (1956); Kessen (1961); Escalona (1962, 1963, 1965); Kagan and Lewis (1965); Fantz (1966); Stechler and Latz (1966); Wolff (1966); Korner and Grobstein (1967); Thomas, Chess, and Birch (1968); Sander (1969, 1975, 1980); M. Lewis (1972); Brazelton (1973, 1974); Korner (1974a); and Anders (1978)—have studied newborn behavior and have speculated about its significance for development. Motility, sensory reactivity, autonomic function, state and state regulation, biological rhythms reflected in sleep-wake and other cycles, visual behavior, and temperamental differences are among the areas of focus. It appears to be a valid assumption that variations in such congenital characteristics influence the process of development and developmental outcome.

The importance of biological endowment has also been emphasized in psychoanalytic developmental psychology in reference to the instinctual drives and to the ego. Freud (1905) proposed that the instinctual drives, including those in the normal range, differ from one individual to another from early on, both in their strength and in their maturation. Following this thought, Alpert, Neubauer, and Weil (1956), studying deviant children, suggested that there are unusual variations in drive endowment that influence the course of a child's development, a view congenial with the clinical experience of others.

Hartmann (1939, 1958), in particular, has called attention to the importance of the inborn apparatuses (somatic and mental) in the development of personality and speaks of them as components of the ego constitution. The apparatuses, reflecting the preadaptedness of the human child, are the expressions of a phylogenetically assured fit with external reality—that is, with an average expectable environment. Among these apparatuses are those that after differentiation become major ego control and executive functions, including motility, perception, intentionality, intelligence, language, memory, delay of discharge, and the synthetic function. One application of Hartmann's propositions lies in the recognition that defects in these apparatuses result in a dyssynchrony between environmental opportunities and demands and tend to interfere with psychological development and adaptation in general. Behavioral disturbances of various kinds may result. A less frequent but significant occurrence is one in which an infant may be able to evoke a supportive environmental response and extract development-promoting experiences despite a defect in the apparatus. Such children are often referred to as relatively invulnerable or resilient.

Thomas, Chess, and Birch (1968) propose that there are differences in temperament, probably operative at birth, that influence how infants and young children behave and how parents react to them. In citing the need for an approach that acknowledges complexity in studies of infant behavior, Cohen (1974) has noted the usefulness of viewing the organization of behavior as an interaction of biological endowment and psychosocial forces and emphasized the effect of early experience. Illustrating the need for an interactional and multivariate model in studies of infant behavior, he writes:

As a result of the genome and prenatal and neonatal experiences, children are born with differing *congenital endowments* . . . and thus differing thresholds for the elicitation and disorganization of congenitally organized behavior. . . . In basic and still unclear ways, congenital endowment and the congenital organization of behavior are patterned by complex biochemical interactions. . . . In turn, the *early experiences* of a child—including nutrition, infection, drugs, and trauma of delivery—lead to enduring patterns of behavior encoded in central nervous system metabolism. For example, appropriate stimulation and optimal stress . . . may condition the nervous system in such a way that later novel situations are neither too overwhelming nor blocked from attention. Arising from the match between the child's endowment and the environment are early adaptations and patterns of response and perception. These persistent early adaptations—such as the habitual fear or anxiety of the child with low threshold for disorganization—shape the child's later adaptations and style of approach to new developmental tasks. Behavioral patterns and hierarchies of action patterns in this way assume a type of autonomy which may become crystallized characteristics of behavior through social reinforcement. [Pp. 386–87]

Maturation and Development

We share the widely accepted view that innate and experiential factors in continuous interaction codetermine development. That is, development, including the development of the mind, proceeds through the interaction of the child's inborn maturing systems (somatic, physiologic, mental) and the forces of the environment. In this process, inborn components and systems are successively called into play according to an inherent biologic timetable and, in interaction with the environment, become organized into what can be called action units or functions that serve adaptation and the learning that is a part of it. The various maturing systems are differentiated and integrated with one another and contribute to the ongoing developmental process (Hartmann 1939, 1958; Hartmann, Kris, and Loewenstein 1946; Benjamin 1961). It is useful, as Hartmann suggests, to distinguish three kinds of developmental processes: those that occur without essential and specific influence from the external world; those that are coordinated to typical experiences, that is, are triggered by average expectable environmental situations; and those that depend upon atypical experience.

In describing developmental functions Hartmann, Kris, and Loewenstein (1946) suggest the usefulness of viewing *maturation* as indicating the processes of growth that occur relatively independent of environmental influences and *development* as indicating those processes in which environment and maturation interact more closely. While maturation processes are not impervious to environmental influences, both normal and adverse, they are relatively independent factors which both during and after birth bring the inborn apparatuses successively into play and determine, at least grossly, the rhythm of developmental processes. In a similar vein, Spitz (1965) describes maturation as the unfolding of inborn functions of the species which emerge in the course of embryonic development or are carried forward after birth and become manifest at later stages in life. He defines development as the emergence of forms, functions, and behavior that are the outcome of exchanges between the organism, on the one hand, and the inner and outer environment, on the other. The clinical usefulness of distinguishing between the definitions of maturation and development has been illustrated by Provence and Lipton (1962) in a study of experientially deprived institutionalized infants in whom maturation in some respects occurred normally while development lagged behind. For example, the approach and grasp patterns of the infants evolved in the expected sequence as described by Halverson (1937) and included in the standardized infant tests. Yet the infants did not utilize these patterns in the expected way to reach out, grasp and manipulate. Similarly the "mama," "baba," "dada" sounds, though sparse in number, emerged at the normal time and yet did not develop specificity in social interchange as names of persons. When development manifestly proceeds without difficulty— that is, silently—the integrity of the maturational process is assumed. But discrepancies between maturation and development, as expressed in the delay or distortion of functions, can be identified in some infants. The recognition of such discrepancies points the way to therapeutic measures that fit the individual child, supporting developmental progress (Provence and Lipton 1962; Provence 1965, 1972, 1978).

One might ask why we were concerned with constructs such as

endowment and maturation in a service-centered study. Such considerations affected our thinking about the importance of antepartum care of the mothers and the influence of their health and nutritional status on their children. While we were not directly involved in antepartum care we encouraged mothers to take advantage of it. In addition, we assisted in alleviating concerns about labor and delivery by showing expectant mothers the delivery suites and answering many questions. In respect to the newborns, the pediatric, behavioral, and neurological examinations of each child provided information about congenital characteristics, including reaction patterns, that we took into account in our view of the child. For example, Chapter 6 describes a newborn who was uncomfortable, disorganized, and difficult to manage and shows how the kind of baby he was influenced our work with his mother. From the beginning, too, we tried to understand the parent's attitudes toward the baby and how these influenced child care and other behavior toward the child. In a continuing way, the pediatric care of the child and aspects of the daycare program reflected our concern first of all with the intactness and functioning of the child's body and second with endowment, maturation, and growth as essentials of healthy psychological development.

Environment and Experience

The term "environment" is used to include aspects of the physical and social world of the infant that define the setting in which he lives. The designation "experience" may well be more useful in considering a specific child's development though it includes much of what is thought of as environment. Escalona (1968) suggests that experience is a useful term because it is subjective and implies an influence of one kind or another. She says:

> By experience and experience patterns we mean the sensations, the body feelings and affective states that the infant feels, and the manner in which fluctations in awareness are linked to perceptual input. . . . The infant's experience comes to include the

psychic processes that accompany and begin to guide his behavior. To the degree to which this is the case, the young child's goals and fears, his established inclinations and aversions, and all forms of ideation (and later thought) are part and parcel of his experience. [P. 62]

In the child-development and clinical literature there are many reports on how subjective experiences of children influence their overall development as well as their attitudes and self-regard. The application of this current knowledge influences preventive and therapeutic programs. When the characteristics of good nurturing care or of an environment that facilitates development are outlined or when adverse environments and events are described, the focus is on the physical surroundings and material objects, the behavior and communications of others, and any other stimuli that are believed to impinge upon the child and influence him in some way.

Congenital characteristics, as indicated earlier, play a role from the beginning in determining what is experienced—that is, what is selectively extracted. Characteristics such as the sensitivity of perceptual apparatuses, the drive toward activity, and other reaction characteristics from early on are shaped, modified, augmented, toned down by the characteristics and responses of the environment. But the infant in turn influences his environment and therefore his own experience, at first primarily through his effect on the caregiver.

How differently an infant who is blind or deaf or who cannot move normally perceives the world compared with a healthy infant. Infants with unusual physiological and psychological sensitivities often seem overwhelmed by ordinary stimuli (Bergmann and Escalona 1949); those who have worked with such children are persuaded that both their somatic and psychic experiences are quite unusual. Vulnerability to developmental problems and departures from ordinary expectable experiences characterize, in general, infants with biological disorders. However, it is also safe to assume that perfectly healthy infants differ in their experiences. For example, Escalona (1963) has presented data on some of the ways in which differences in the activity levels of infants and in their mothers' style of child care resulted in differing experiences that influenced the infants' individual development. Her data support the hypothesis that "very different actions on the part of mothers (or other environmental variations) may have similar consequences in terms of their impact upon the child's experience, as reflected in behavior; and conversely, that similar or identical external stimulation may have varying and opposite consequences . . . in terms of the direction in which they alter behavior. Two categories of variables, environmental and organismic, converge and reciprocally interact in shaping the moment-by-moment and year-by-year experience of the growing child" (p. 242).

Other determinants of the influence of a particular environmental factor or event are developmental-phase characteristics and antecedent experiences in the child's life. Level of development and phase-specific tendencies (vulnerabilities, skills, characteristics of thought, psychodynamic constellations, cognitive style, perceptual modalities, and so forth) will partly determine what is experienced. The prehistory of the child as related to any specific situation is also important. For example, an event in the child's life such as temporary separation from the mother at a specific period will have been preceded by many transactions with her that have influenced the strength of the relationship, the perception and stability of the child's mental representations, the degree of distress he feels in her absence, his ability to accept a substitute, and his capacity to cope with change or stress.

Finally, the immediate situation of the child and the nature of the stimulus or event are relevant in what is experienced—for example, the intensity, duration, and timing of a specific event in respect to the child's physiological and psychological state at a given time on a specific day. Both theory and common sense tell us that what an adult chooses to do with or for a child will be influenced by the child's mood, state of comfort or discomfort, fatigue, readiness for interaction, and a host of other things that are most clearly discerned by the adult who knows the child well.

In respect to planning daycare and other programs for young children there are two general levels at which the concept of experience requires consideration. First, what general plans would one make based on knowledge of what children of a particular age are likely to need for their physical care and health and to facilitate development? Second, within that general framework, how would one individualize plans in accordance with the current developmental characteristics and needs of a particular child? In a daycare center the first level involves such plans as the physical space for children, selection of appropriate toys and activities, provision of an adequate number of nurturing adults, and so on. It is at the second level, that of individualization, that the meaning of experience for a specific child must be taken into account if one is to respond most appropriately to his interests and needs.

Granted the individual differences among infants, they are similar enough in their biological attributes and in their developmental characteristics and needs, and the average expectable environment is well enough defined by culture and child-rearing traditions, to permit at least an approximate definition of experiences that are likely to support development and adaptation in a general way. But it remains important, especially in the development of programs for children living in adverse environments and for biologically vulnerable children, to recognize that the *individual* child's experience requires close attention.

Much of the report of the project is about the attention paid to providing an environment and experiences for child and parent that would be supportive and facilitating and would alleviate stress and suffering.

The Phase or Stage Concept

The developmental phase or stage concept in the broad sense means that there are developmental trends that, on the average, converge at a given time and in characteristic ways. The concept includes behavioral norms as well as the idea of characteristic dynamic constellations and regulatory mechanisms of the mind. Typical developmental tasks are mastered during particular phases and, in general, typical capabilities, vulnerabilities, attitudes, conflicts, perceptions, modes of thought characterize children at specific ages.

Deviations in timing or the occurrence of atypical phases may result from any one of the factors that influence development in general. Phenomena may make a precocious appearance or may lag behind the usual timetable. Moreover, an experience that was of little relevance in one phase of development may be of great significance in another.

The stages of psychosexual development as outlined in psychoanalytic theory (Freud 1905) exemplify the phase concept. The common causes of anxiety in early childhood are related to these stages (Freud 1926, Kris 1950, Benjamin 1963, Spitz 1950). Erikson's epigenetic theory (1953, 1959) describes a sequence of phases of psychosocial development and relates them to psychosexual development. Each phase of the life cycle is assumed to be characterized by a specific primary or central developmental task that must be solved during that phase, though the solution is prepared in previous phases and is further worked out in subsequent ones. The theory conceives of the sequence of epigenetic phases as universal and of the typical solutions as varying from society to society. Other examples of the phase concept include the subphases of the separation-individuation process outlined by Mahler and her colleagues (1975), the stages of sensorimotor intelligence as defined by Piaget (1952), the ages and stages of childhood described by Gesell et al. (1940), and the behavior norms organized into developmental tests.

Phase-specific tendencies, as indicated earlier, will partly determine the impact on development of a given experience. The child's reaction at a particular level also has a historical basis in that it is determined by previous growth and development. For example, pathogenic vulnerability to anxiety may find expression in ways specific to a given level even though the vulnerability can be traced to biological endowment or to factors of growth or environment that marked earlier phases of a child's development. Thus a specific event may cause a degree of stress that impedes development; at another time the same event may call forth an adaptive response that stimulates development and enlarges the scope of the child's functioning.

The phase concept most commonly affects the work of early childhood specialists, as it did this project, by the way in which it influences assessment of the child and the choice of experiences and services provided. It is part of what is implied in offering a program geared to developmental needs. The assumption is that there are optimal periods for each step in learning, adjustment, integration, and overcoming conflicts. That being the case, child-rearing practices, education, socialization and training experiences of all kinds, and aspects of medical care must, in order to be most effective, take into account what is known about phase specificity and its antecedents. The phase concept influences the counseling of parents, providing them a tool to understand their child more completely and respond in ways that support the child's development. Specific examples in which the concept is used include advice about how to provide child care and education in a positive sense and how to protect the child as much as possible from experiences judged to be excessively depriving, stressful, traumatic, or frankly noxious. The phase concept also influences views about the parent-child relationship and the development of parenthood. Specific phase characteristics in the child interact with parental attitudes, nurturing talents, coping abilities, and unresolved conflicts in ways that can have a profound influence on the behavior of each and on the relationship. The useful application of this concept requires consideration of each child's uniqueness with regard to tolerances, strengths, weaknesses, and temperamental characteristics.

Parenthood as a Developmental Process

From experience with healthy young parents and with troubled parents and their children, we have been impressed with the usefulness of viewing parenthood as a developmental process and stage of life. This view has been presented with especial clarity by Erikson (1953, 1959) and Benedek (1959), who emphasize that parenthood is characterized by new developmental tasks, vulnerabilities, and potentialities for conflict as well as new areas of satisfaction and fulfillment. Pregnancy and prospective parenthood, as Bibring et al. (1961) point out, is a normal developmental crisis imposing new adaptive tasks. Pregnancy involves profound endocrine, general somatic, and psychological changes. As a major turning point in life, especially for the young primipara, pregnancy brings about some disturbance of personality equilibrium even in the relatively healthy person, including the emergence of unresolved conflicts or of improved mastery of earlier developmental phases and tasks. As noted by Bibring (1959, 1961), Erikson (1953), and Naylor (1970), the crisis of pregnancy, like the crises of puberty and menopause, provides a testing ground of psychological health. The repeated opportunities to advance or the failure to advance lead either to new developmental achievements or to maladaptive solutions. In the case of pregnancy, maladaptive solutions are likely to have adverse effects on parental attitudes and behavior.

The attitudes of parents toward the growing child are influenced by many factors in their previous experience, by current realities in the life situation, including the relationship of the couple, and by the characteristics of the child himself. In the parent the process of adaptation is powerfully stimulated by contact with the newborn, and parental attitudes toward the child are continuously influenced by the child's growth and development. Changing needs and demands of the child stimulate different reactions in the parents. Their ability to adapt their attitudes and behavior in accordance with the child's development and changing needs is one of the indicators of developmental progress in the parents. In discussing these issues Coleman, Kris, and Provence (1953) indicate that, for example, a mother who delights in her infant may react with irritation when he moves toward greater autonomy and independence. The reverse also occurs: a child who has become independent may gain admiration from a mother who did not enjoy the care of her infant at an earlier age. Other well known intolerances and sensitive points for parents related to the child's development are issues around negativism, separation, sphincter control, aggressive behavior, and sexual curiosity; these account in some instances for acute parent-child conflict.

Beyond general adaptive abilities, how well the tasks of parenthood are carried out may be clarified in part by our understanding of the kind of care each parent received as a child and how well the conflicts of earlier phases of development have been resolved. While the child's struggle to work through the vulnerabilities and conflicts of each phase often reactivates in the parent unresolved problems of the same phase of development, it is also an opportunity for the parent to work on these problems again, and the result may be a new level of personality integration characterized by greater maturity and feelings of well-being (Benedek 1959).

Planning for services in the project was based in part on the view of parenthood as a potentially difficult and challenging stage of life but one offering a new identity and the possibility of a sense of achievement and fulfullment as well as pleasure in being a parent. The choice of services was based on the realization that those eligible for admission to the study were deprived of many of the supports that make child care and other aspects of daily life less difficult. It was anticipated, therefore, that in addition to whatever conflicts each might experience as parents, they were all under varying degrees of inner and outer stress. Helping parents to select appropriate challenges, reduce undesirable stresses, and increase their capacity to cope with future stress was a goal related to enabling them to function in ways that would promote their own development and that of their children.

The Central Role of Human Relationships

We share the view that human relationships are crucially important for their influence on a child's physical, mental, and emotional development and his coming to function in the society of which he is a part. The nature of those relationships during early childhood exerts a powerful influence on behavior at any given moment as well as on future development. This view has been put forward especially by psychoanalytic developmental psychology, which assigns central importance to the child's relationships with parent figures.

The human infant is predisposed by inborn characteristics to become attached to his caregivers; that is, there is a readiness for social contact that is coordinated with the responsiveness of the caretaking adults to the infant's needs and with phase-specific needs of their own. Both Erikson's psychosocial theory (1953, 1959) and Hartmann's adaptation theory (1939, 1958) assume an inborn coordination to an average expectable environment; as Rapaport (1959) emphasizes, these two theories trace "the unfolding of the genetically social character of the human individual in the course of his encounters with the social environment at each phase of his epigenesis" (p. 15). Erikson's concept of mutuality specifies that the crucial coordination is between the developing individual and his human (social) environment, and that this coordination is mutual. Recent studies of the origins of reciprocity in maternal-infant interaction (Brazelton et al. 1974) bear upon the mutuality of the adaptation from the beginning. Erikson's (1964) felicitous words convey much that is significant in this regard:

> A seeming paradox of human life is man's collective power to create his own environment, although each individual is born with a naked vulnerability extending into a prolonged infantile dependence. The weakness of the newborn, however, is truly relative. While far removed from any measure of mastery over the physical world, newborn man is endowed with an appearance and with responses which appeal to the tending adults' tenderness and make them wish to attend to his needs; which arouse concern in those who are concerned with his well-being; and which, in making adults care, stimulate their active caretaking. . . . Defenseless as babies are, they have mothers at their command, families to protect the mothers, societies to support the structure of families, and traditions to give a cultural continuity to systems of te. _ing and training. [P. 114–15]

The influences of the society and culture are carried and mediated at first by the caretaking persons. Following the thought of Erikson and Hartmann, Rapaport's (1959) definition seems valid: "Thus it is not assumed that societal norms are grafted upon the genetically social individual by 'disciplines' and 'socialization,' but that the society into which the individual is born makes him its member by influencing the manner in which he solves the tasks imposed by each phase of his epigenetic development" (p. 15).

The study of human object relations has been a focus of psycho-analysis from the beginning. Freud (1926) outlines two stages in their development: the first stage, in which the infant relates to the need-satisfying, comfort-giving object, and the later stage of the permanent object—that is, the stage of object constancy. Many psycho-analytic clinicians and investigators—among them Hartmann, Kris, and Loewenstein (1946); Kris (1950, 1951); Hartmann (1952); Winnicott (1960); Jacobson (1964); A. Freud (1965); Spitz (1965); and Mahler, Pine, and Bergmann (1975)—have contributed to the literature on these two overlapping phases and have identified sub-phases within them. The prolonged dependency of the human child, his need for care and protection not only for survival but for experiences highly significant for development and learning, intensifies the importance of the child's nurturers and their influence on development. A mother's relationship to her infant is both biological and social. Endocrine, hormonal, and other physiological changes that are part of pregnancy, childbirth, and the postpartum period help to prepare her for motherhood. At the same time the experience of pregnancy places great demands for psychological adaptation on her and on the baby's father. The baby's social and emotional needs are met in close association with his bodily needs; it is believed that the child begins to form his first attachment to the person who is able to understand and satisfy his basic needs. The importance of continuity and consistency of the maternal figure to optimize development is generally agreed upon in psychoanalysis. Anna Freud (1965), summarizing much that has been learned from clinical investigation, emphasizes that interference with the mother-infant tie from any cause or failure of the mother to play her part as the reliable, need-fulfilling, and comfort-giving person may interfere with the child's subsequent development in a variety of ways. Psychoanalytic theory also notes that the mother, who is the provider of many experiences of comfort, stimulation, and pleasure for the child, is also the source of limits, prohibitions, discomfort, and frustrations in the normal course of their daily life together and that all of these experiences in combination are important for the child's healthy development. The education and guidance that are a part of the socialization process must include prohibitions and frustrations as well as stimulation, comfort, and pleasure, and the prohibitions and frustrations facilitate the infant's development if they are carried out in an atmosphere of loving attention (Hartmann, Kris, and Loewenstein 1946). The growing literature on father-infant relationships has sharpened awareness that nurturing the young is a parental function, not limited to mothers (Benedek 1970; Abelin 1975; Gurwitt 1976; Lamb 1976; Herzog 1980).

There is an interdependence of object relations, ego, and drive development. For example, the baby's ability first to recognize the mother and others and later to "read" nonverbal cues or to understand speech always involves significant cognitive elements. The child's perception, intelligence, and discriminatory abilities are involved in his relationships with others from the beginning. Similarly in terms of interdependence it is believed that the infant's drive endowment and its differentiation determine in part his individual needs and behavior, including aspects of his interaction with others, and that the quality of his relationships facilitates or interferes with drive development and organization.

The benevolence, reliability, and continuity of the nurturing persons are important also because such care stimulates specific dimensions of development (Provence 1977). Such mental functions as the child's discrimination between things and persons in the environment, his coming to distinguish between his inner and outer worlds, and his interest in objects and activities depend in important ways on the quality of his relationships with others. Motility, perception, speech, and intelligence as autonomous ego functions may be enhanced or impeded according to the nature of the psychosocial environment. The child's awareness of and attitudes toward reality are strongly influenced by object relations, and trouble in object relations often interferes with the formation of stable defenses, another important function of the ego. The development of the affective life and its expression, differentiation, and intensity are very sensitive to parental behavior and other aspects of the social environment.*

---

*Another influential theoretical position is that of Bowlby and Ainsworth and their colleagues. They deal with concepts of attachment and attachment behavior. As

The child's interest in and use of inanimate objects during the early years of life are also influenced by his human object relationships. On the basis of studies of severely deprived infants in foundling homes, Katherine Wolf (1948) concluded that the infant's coming to believe in inanimate objects (a world of things)—that is, to have a memory of their consistency and constancy—depends upon the consistency and constancy of the human objects. In this hypothesis, Wolf integrated propositions from psychoanayltic theory and from Piaget's theory of the development of intelligence, especially the establishment of object permanence. Later investigations, including a study of experientially deprived infants in institutions (Provence and Ritvo 1961, Provence and Lipton 1962), provided data that supported Wolf's view. The relationship between infant and parent figures is an important source of the infant's interest in toys, and the parents' pleasure in the baby's activity with the toy further promotes his own pleasure in it. Parental investment also adds to the momentum and elaboration of self-initiated activities and motivation. Those who observe infants and young children are familiar with how an adult's enthusiasm for a toy or an activity makes it attractive to the child. Such knowledge is used frequently in stimulating the interest of the child who is apathetic or indifferent, or whom one wants to help with learning or with play. The influence of the child's relationship with the mother and other trustworthy persons on playful activity, both social play and play with toys, has

---

Ainsworth and Bell (1970) state, "The term [attachment] as originally introduced by Bowlby (1958, 1969) and as used by Ainsworth (1963, 1964, 1967), implies an ethological and evolutionary viewpoint, and hence has connotations not necessarily shared by those with other theoretical orientations." An attachment is defined as an affectional tie that one person forms with another *specific* person—a tie that endures over time. Attachment *behaviors* are those which promote proximity or contact. Once an attachment has been formed, its intensity may be heightened or diminished by situational conditions but is not viewed as vanishing during periods when attachment behavior is not evident. Ainsworth and Bell emphasize that the individual's predisposition to seek intermittent proximity to the object of attachment has an inner, structural basis. Attachment theory and object relations theory obviously have certain similarities but, as Ainsworth warns, they have very different connotations. This cautionary note is important, since some of the child development literature suggests that the two are interchangeable and synonymous.

significant application to child care and education and to clinical work with young children. More is said of this later in this chapter in the section on play.

Studies of newborn infants and of newborns and their parents have extended and made more explicit some of the knowledge clinicians have relied upon in considering the nature of the early parent-child relationship. For example, studies by Sander (1962, 1969, 1970) with newborns and their mothers deal with the influence of each upon the other's behavior. In a recent paper Sander (1980) demonstrates how events between infant and caregiver assume importance in terms of their temporal organization and how well they are synchronized. He has studied the process of "fitting together" by which adapted interaction is achieved at a given moment, and he proposes that the *process* of fitting together brings about the connection between the newborn infant and the caregiver. Elsewhere Sander (1962, 1964, 1975) has described the changing organization of events and interactions over the first three years of life as a sequence of levels of fitting together of infant and caregiver and suggests that the context of mutual familiarity between mother and child during the first eighteen months sets the stage for fitting together on the next, more subtle level of thought and inner perception, involving the "reading" of intentionality, feeling states, emotional expression, and so forth. Similarly, studies by Brazelton and his colleagues (1974) having to do with mother-infant and father-infant interactions demonstrate complexity even in the early days of life. Stern (1971) has documented some of the subtleties of how mothers and young infants make and avoid eye contact and influence each other with exchanges of such brief duration that they might pass unnoticed in ordinary observation. Of relevance, too, for the understanding of human relationships are studies that illustrate that from the beginning the infant is an active contributor to social interaction and influences the relationship in a variety of ways (Korner 1965, 1974b; Stern 1974; Brazelton 1974; Brazelton et al. 1974; Lewis and Lee-Painter 1974; Emde et al. 1976; Emde 1980). That the infant exerts a powerful influence on his parents has long been recognized by clinicians attuned to the complexities of the developmental process and, in a commonsense way, by almost everyone. Nonetheless, the studies cited above, many of them utilizing the newer technologies, are fine examples of the more precise ways in which the dynamic, interactional dyadic relationship can be described and its significance appreciated.

Some experiences are known to delay or interfere with the establishment of mother-infant attachment in the early weeks of life. Leiderman and Seashore (1975), studying healthy premature babies and their mothers, found significant differences in the early mother-child relationship between those in which baby and mother were separated early and those in which mothers had early contact as caregivers. The work of Klaus and Kennell (1976) has emphasized the importance to the mother-child relationship of the active support of physicians, nurses, and other hospital personnel in facilitating the beginning attachment of mother and baby. Such work is reminiscent of the pioneering demonstration and research project of Edith Jackson and her colleagues in the Rooming-In Project at Yale in the 1940s and 50s (Jackson and Klatskin 1950). Much of the activity of that project was based on the assumption that a benevolent and supportive environment, provided by skilled clinicians, could make a difference in how parents understood and nurtured their young children from the beginning and in how they developed as parents.

The many studies on separation from and loss of parents also provide constructs that show the importance of human relationships for the child's development. Studies of infants without families, of children who have lost one parent through death, divorce, or illness, of children in disorganized families and in multiple placements, and of children with psychotic parents are examples (Freud and Burlingham 1944; Goldfarb 1945; Spitz 1945, 1946, 1950; Spitz and Wolf 1946; Bowlby 1951, 1973; Provence and Lipton 1962; Benjamin 1963; Yarrow 1964; Mahler 1966; Pavenstedt et al. 1967; Anthony 1970; Goldstein, Freud, and Solnit 1973; Furman 1974; Wallerstein and Kelly 1975, 1980). There is little disagreement about the fact that separation or loss has an impact on the child's psychological development. The questions to be addressed both theoretically and in each individual case concern the extent of the influence, the specific aspects of the child's mental and emotional life affected,

the issues of vulnerability and resilience, and the effect of such experiences on subsequent development.

A belief in the significance of human relationships for the child's
development strongly influenced the project, including the emphasis
we placed on facilitating and supporting the parent-child relationship and on providing good substitute care. For example, it determined the number of infants assigned to each caregiver-teacher, the
careful selection of that adult, and the attention given to assuring
continuity of care. Other influences on various aspects of the work
with child and parent are spelled out in later chapters.

We also believed that the effectiveness of the effort for each family
would be strongly influenced by the relationships developed between specific staff members and parents; that is, the development
of an effective working alliance would be related to the continuity of
interaction and the parents' perception of the trustworthiness of staff
as well as to staff competence. In addition, we were aware that, in a
group effort such as this one, respect and trust among staff members
would make a great difference in how the work proceeded and that
planning must include attention to staff relationships. This attitude
recognized that the supportive environment for parents and infants
was emotionally toned—that the emotional climate influenced effectiveness. This has been discussed in detail in *The Challenge of Daycare* (Provence, Naylor, and Patterson 1977).

The importance of separation to both parents and young children
led us to devote much attention to assisting them with their feelings
about separation. This came up most often, but not exclusively, with
those using the daycare service. An example of an acute separation
problem is given in the case reports of Miss Galer and Steven (Chapter
4). The case of Miss Keeler and Greg (Chapter 7) illustrates a more
chronic one.

Physical Care of the Child

The kind of care the child receives affects much more than his physical health. General learning and psychosocial development are also

influenced by the nature of the care. For the infant and very young child, feeding, bathing, cleaning, diapering, and dressing are events around which many social, cognitive, and affective communications come from the caregiver via her voice, her face, her touch. Very early, her interest in him, concern for his comfort, and pleasure in being with him begin to be transmitted in these ordinary caring situations. Her handling may be gentle or rough, intrusive or adaptive to the child; it may reflect the mutuality of the relationship or its opposite. The child's body and its boundaries, its feelings and sensations, and the person and actions of the caregiver in the social context are the most frequent and influential sources of his earliest learning experiences. The first stages in the development of the sense of self, of a personal identity, involve awareness of the body self. Schilder (1935, 1950) emphasized that all sensations the infant experiences are of significance in the image of the body. The sensations of the surface of the body, of the muscles and viscera and erogenous zones, and the sensations that accompany such actions as perception, grasping, moving, and sucking have an influence upon the infant's development of awareness of the body self: "there is no question that our own activity is insufficient to build up the image of the own body. The touches of others, the interest of others in different parts of our body, will be of enormous importance in development of the postural model of the body" (p. 126). Psychoanalytic theory emphasizes the psychobiological nature of early ego development, pointing out that the ego is at first a body ego; self-awareness in the mental sense follows self-awareness in the body sense.

The care the child receives and the attitudes of the caregivers toward his body strongly influence his later sense of identity and feelings of self-worth. For example, when the child is old enough to walk, to run, to climb, to move out toward his environment, he at first has little judgment about realistic dangers and may protest adults' limiting and protecting him when he is pursuing some attractive but dangerous object or activity. But protected in a calm and supportive manner he learns eventually to distinguish between what is safe and what is dangerous. The expectation that the important adults will keep him from harm is a characteristic of the well-cared-for young child and is one important aspect of his feeling valued. He also benefits from seeing others being cared for: When another child is ill or hurt, young children feel concerned and are reassured when that child is comforted or his injuries are taken care of—even while they may also feel jealous of the added attention he receives. Moreover, such experiences in regard to another help a child begin to feel empathic with the injured child and to identify with the actions and attitudes of the caregiver, enhancing socialization.

Another relevant aspect of caring for the child's body has to do with encounters with aggressive behavior and with his own hostile feelings as they emerge in his transactions with others. Protecting the child's body from the aggression of others and in turn preventing him from aggressing too strongly against others convey interest in him. They also convey an attitude that favorably influences his development toward control of his own impulses.

The provision of good physical and health care was an essential aspect of the intervention project and proved at every stage to be of great importance both for the health of the child and for our relationship with parents. We held the strong conviction that continuity of health care of the children by a primary physician would be indispensable in helping parents with their child's health, building their confidence in themselves as parents, enabling them to utilize the services provided by the project to the fullest extent they chose, and assuring them of their value as human beings. The health care was carried out primarily by the pediatricians of the staff and secondarily, for the children who were in daycare, by the caregiver-teachers, including nurses. It was amply documented that our concern for the children's physical well-being in the ways described had great meaning for their parents. For the children in daycare there was no doubt that the staff's commitment to good physical care went far toward alleviating parental anxiety about the long hours they were separated from their children. It was a tangible demonstration of interest and concern. For example, the staff's practice of letting a parent know how the child had eaten or slept and discussing any sign of illness or minor injury was reassuring. Also, the fact that infants and toddlers were dressed in fresh clothing following their afternoon naps and bathed when this was needed, and the staff's obvious pleasure in dressing the children and preparing them for the return of their parents in the afternoon communicated, perhaps more effectively than words, a degree of interest and affection for the children that had great meaning for the parents.

The probability is that our working relationship with the parents, though it developed in intensity and kind somewhat differently in each individual instance, was enormously enhanced by the fact that from the beginning we provided health care for the children. Moreover, that this health care was closely integrated with the other services and that the services as a whole were provided by a small number of persons whom the parents came to know were also, in our view, very important determinants of the utilization of the services.

Play and the Young Child's Development

Play has an important function in the development of the infant and young child. Of the vast literature on the subject contributed by persons with widely divergent interests, most relevant in the present context are ideas about the function of play in the child's cognitive development and mental health, the style and content of play as indicative of the course and vicissitudes of mental development, and play as a medium of communication with the child and as a diagnostic and therapeutic modality.

Greenacre (1969) comments on the probable biological advantage in play and the maturational pressures that influence it. "It affords room," she says, "for new departures especially valuable in animals whose adult life demands plasticity and resourcefulness." "It seems," she continues, "however, that play cannot occur by maturation alone, that it requires some liberating stimulus from the environment and is susceptible to the impingement of a variety of stimuli. . . . The biological significance of play is partly a safety valve for overflowing energy, partly an expression of imitativeness, partly a correlate of agreeable feelings, but mainly an irresponsible apprenticeship for adult activities and an opportunity for testing new departures" (p. 356).

Waelder (1932) stresses the importance of play for the child in reducing anxiety through its role in mastering those situations that cause anxiety. Greenacre (1959) too has commented on the anxiety-reducing role of play: "Play, being under the child's direction, can represent fragments of reality according to his needs and wishes. Thus he can dose himself with larger or smaller bits and need not bring the whole overwhelming situation down on himself at one time, even in played-out forms" (p. 66). Greenacre also emphasizes the functional pleasure of play, a term introduced by Karl Bühler (1929) referring to a sense of pleasure in performance without regard to the success of a specific activity.

Hartmann (1939, 1958) has commented on the function of play as an example that the child's relation to reality is in part learned by detours, that there are avenues of adaptation to reality that at first lead away from the real situation. Both play and fantasy as examples of this process function in part as preparation for reality and may lead to better mastery of it.

Erikson (1964) speaks of the evolutionary necessity for representational play in order that the child can "learn to bind together an inner and outer world, a remembered past and an anticipated future, before he can learn to master the tools used in cooperation [and] the roles distributed in the community." He proposes that "play is to the child what thinking, planning, and blueprinting are to the adult, a trial universe in which conditions are simplified and methods exploratory, so that past failures can be thought through, expectations tested. . . . In the toy world the child plays out the past, often in disguised form, in the manner of dreams, and he begins to master the future by anticipating it in countless variations and repetitive themes" (p. 120).

Piaget (1951, 1969) has had much to say about play, especially the importance of symbolic play. It is indispensable to the affective and intellectual equilibrium, Piaget and Inhelder (1969) propose, that the young child "have available to him an area of activity whose motivation is . . . assimilation of reality to the self without coercion or sanctions. Such an area is play" (p. 58). The systems of symbols characteristic of play provide a means of self-expression constructed by the child and capable of being bent to his wishes.

The comments of Murphy (1972) on patterns of play seen in children are similar to those of others in reflecting on both cognitive and affective factors. These patterns "are individually shaped by wishes, angers, fears, conflicts, worries but they also reveal puzzlement, questions, the need to clarify experience, to make a cognitive map or to improve on nature" (p. 121). Murphy emphasizes, as do Erikson and Piaget, the creative nature of play and its role in problem solving and the resolution of conflicts, among other benefits.

It is well known to clinicians and educators that a young child who does not play is a child in trouble. The earliest forms of playful activity are part of the interaction of infant and mother, and the first steps in its development are stimulated by the social interchanges between them. Infants deprived of such interchanges do not become normally playful (Provence and Lipton 1962). The first toys provided are often placed in or suspended over the crib for the baby to look at and later to reach for. But the earliest playthings are parts of the baby's own body and that of his mother. Anchored in the social interaction and strongly influenced by the maturation of somatic apparatuses, playful activity proceeds, gaining a momentum and differentiation of its own and becoming increasingly complex.

Characteristics of play in a specific child also provide information that reflects his personality characteristics, cognitive development, anxieties and areas of conflict, as well as his efforts to cope with stress, defend against danger, and adapt to his environment. Playful interaction between parents and child (or its absence) provides clues to the quality of the parent-child relationship. Diagnostic and therapeutic measures for infants and young children with developmental difficulties involve the use of play as a medium of communication. Activation of the child through play is an essential part of the treatment of delayed or disturbed development.

A belief in the importance of play in the young child's life led us to devote much thought, time, and energy to creating an environment and a psychological atmosphere that facilitated playful activity in general and for individual children in particular. Children in daycare and toddler school had adults available who arranged appropriate play experiences for individuals and small groups and facilitated play in a variety of ways, including being play partners. Some of the ways in which this was approached and carried out are described in detail in *The Challenge of Daycare*. Examples are included in Appendix 1. The work with parents included helping them to value the play of their children. In addition, as one would expect, observations of the style, level, and content of play of individual children were important aspects of the data. In these days, when it is fashionable to emphasize cognitive development, it should be underscored that play does not exist in a vacuum—it depends on the nature of the human object relationships, on feeling safe and wanted and on the psychological presence of the reassuring, approving parental person.

Learning, Coping, and Adaptation

Among the characteristics of young children who are developing well are an interest in learning, an ability to make efforts to cope with stress, and motivation to engage in transactions with the environment leading to mastery. These are aspects of adaptation, the process through which man comes to terms with his environment.

Hartmann's monograph *Ego Psychology and the Problem of Adaptation* (1958) laid the groundwork and opened the way for the coordination of theories and empirical data regarding adaptation. The fields of developmental psychology and early childhood education have been influenced especially by the writings of Hartmann, Kris, and Loewenstein (1946) and Kris (1950, 1951) on adaptive processes in ego functioning and development, and by Robert White's conceptualization of effectance motivation and competence (1959). Hartmann emphasized the concept of the ego as the means of adjustment to the environment and stressed the special importance of social relationships in the child's adaptation. He pointed out that the human infant is born with rather meager instinct equipment compared with other species and must acquire many of his adaptation processes through learning. The family normally provides the setting in which early learning takes place. But while the child adapts to his environment, he also, through his actions, helps to create that environment. Hartmann, Kris, and Loewenstein (1946) note that psychoanalytic hypotheses regarding learning in infancy "take mainly four factors into account: first, the stage of maturation of the apparatus; second, the reaction of the environment; third, the tolerance [of the child] for deprivation; and fourth, the various types of gratification afforded by processes of learning and the satisfactions that can be obtained as a consequence of mastery" (p. 43).

The beneficial role of experiences of mastery in the child's adaptation was emphasized by White in his 1959 paper "Motivation Reconsidered: The Concept of Competence." White notes that, especially in man, to whom so little is innately provided and who has so much to learn about dealing with the environment, effectance motivation (competence) has high adaptive value. He states that effectance motivation involves satisfactions in which behavior has an exploratory, varying, experimental character and produces changes in the stimulus field: "visual exploration, grasping, crawling and walking, attention and perception, language and thinking, exploring novel objects and places, manipulating the surroundings, and producing effective changes in the environment . . . they all form part of the process whereby the animal or child learns to interact effectively with his environment" (p. 329). More recent studies by Harter and Zigler (1974), Burton White (1975), L. Yarrow and his colleagues (1975, 1976), and Harter (1978) have contributed further to views on the origins of competence in the child, motivation for mastery, and relationships between motivation and cognition. Yarrow (1981) says, "Having an environment in which adults both sensitively respond to the child's needs and provide responsive materials is likely to be most facilitative of mastery" (p. 4).

Lois Murphy's studies of coping, begun around 1952 at the Menninger Foundation, brought another dimension to the understanding of the infant's adaptation. In a 1974 essay on coping, vulnerability, and resilience in childhood, Murphy described the development of her studies. "The concept of coping focusses on what the child is trying to do. In itself it does not imply success but effort. Defensive maneuvers can be part of coping processes. . . . Thus we see coping as a process, involving effort, on the way towards solution of the

problem, as contrasted with ready-made adaptational devices such
as reflexes or, on the other hand, with complete and automatized
mastery and resulting competence" (p. 75). Murphy emphasizes that
coping begins at birth and that there are individual differences in
coping resources. As the infant and child confront new opportunities and experience obstacles, frustrations, and dangers, they must
learn to manage both their inner sensations, feelings, and resources
and the occurrences and demands of the outer environment. Success
in these challenges often brings feelings of mastery (expressed in
behavior) that stimulate further coping efforts. For Murphy, as for
Robert White, coping involves original, imaginative, and innovative
behavior. Murphy's concept also includes the notion that special coping
problems are involved at sensitive periods, another way of discussing phase-specific tasks and vulnerabilities.

Escalona's studies of infancy have also contributed to the understanding of learning and other adaptive ego processes in infant development. She emphasizes the importance of stable patterns of experience in normal development. In a 1963 paper she brings together
aspects of ego psychology and Piaget's work on the development of
intelligence. She recounts that Piaget (1952) demonstrated the
manner in which formal aspects of early experience (sensory motor
schemes) lead to adaptations that take into account properties and
relationships of the real physical world which, once they find mental
representation, constitute the basic elements of thought. She says,

> Such functions or "operations" as anticipation, intentionality,
> means-end relationships, the constancy of the object world, spa-
> tial and temporal coordinates, and the like are, in a manner of
> speaking, "learned" on a sensory motor level, at first without a
> counterpart in terms of corresponding ideas or structures on a
> psychological level. . . . My data suggest the possibility that what
> Piaget proposes for cognition is true of all adaptive aspects of
> mental functioning: namely, that the emergence of such func-
> tions as communication, modulation of affect, control over ex-
> citation, delay and aspects of object relation, and hence identi-
> fication, all are the result of a developmental sequence in sensory

motor terms, before they can emerge as ego functions in the narrower sense. [P. 198]

Escalona's premise is compatible with empirical data from therapeutic work with infants and toddlers. We and others have noted the beneficial effect of activating infants suffering from delayed development through selective stimulation in a supportive, benevolent context. This effect is most conspicuous in those suffering from deficits in the environment—deprivation, inconsistency, discontinuity, confusion, and so forth—but is also seen in infants with sensory defects and other handicaps. (Provence and Lipton 1962; Brazelton et al. 1971; Provence 1972, 1978; Ferholt and Provence 1976; Fraiberg 1971, 1977; Fraiberg et al. 1969.) If one links Piaget's thesis that the infant's physically manipulating objects—that is, "hefting" them—is a necessary condition for the development of intelligence during the sensory motor period and Escalona's suggestion that other adaptive ego processes are also "learned" via a sensory motor sequence, it follows that the child's acting upon the environment is a necessary precondition of many aspects of learning in infancy and early childhood. Besides the obvious activity of sensory and motor systems, here are included the activities that involve social, intellectual, and affective functions. Provence's hypothesis (1974) regarding relationships between activity and vulnerability in infancy is relevant in this context: "The proposition, derived from clinical observations in research and practice, is that unusual inactivity in infancy due to biological or experiential factors or to combinations of both, is a frequent characteristic of the psychologically vulnerable child and, further, that therapy which enables the child to be active in his own behalf reduces symptomatic behavior, enhances general developmental competence, increases coping behavior, and leads to decreased vulnerability" (p. 160).

The foregoing material on the importance of learning in the child's adaptation processes and the significance of experiences of coping and mastery has direct relevance for practices believed to be of special importance in the young child's development. These are, in general, subsumed under the broad heading of "developmental needs."

In our program, the translation of principles into practice concerned the child-care advice and guidance given the parents as well as the specifics of pediatric care and the program of care and education.

In regard to early education, the philosophy that is built upon the inseparability of cognitive and affective development is congenial with our views of how young children learn and the vital role of learning in their lives. This approach has been especially well articulated in the developmental-interaction approach associated with the Bank Street College of Education (Biber and Franklin 1967, Shapiro and Biber 1972, and Biber 1977). The premises of this philosophy of education, which has been evolving for about six decades, have been derived from continuous study of advancing knowledge in the field of child development. A central tenet of the developmental-interaction approach is that "the growth of cognitive functions—acquiring and ordering information, judging, reasoning, problem solving, using systems of symbols—cannot be separated from the growth of personal and interpersonal processes, the development of self-esteem and a sense of identity, internalization and impulse control, capacity for autonomous response, relatedness to other people" (Shapiro and Biber 1972).

This philosophy flows from three main sources: (1) psychodynamic theory, especially the work of those concerned with autonomous ego processes; (2) the psychological theories of those concerned primarily with cognitive development; and (3) educational theorists and practitioners. Fundamental to educational planning and to translating theory into practice are six formulations, here paraphrased in condensed form from Biber (1977): (1) the existence in the child of autonomous ego processes propelled by motivations independent of instinctual drives, but dependent in important measure on the qualities of support, restraint, and stimulation in the environment; (2) the importance of action as a mode of learning, including the role of exercising skills and the regeneration of motivation to activity through pleasure in mastery; (3) the normal occurrence of moments of equilibrium and of instability; (4) the child's tendency to employ at the same time both more primitive and more advanced functional patterns (that is, "mixed" rather than "fixed" levels); (5)

the concept of the self as both image and instrument (that is, not only the process of differentiation of self from the other, but the child's internalized view of his own skills); (6) the fact that growth and normal maturing involve conflict and that conflict resolution bears the imprint of interaction with the salient figures and demands of the culture. This implies the capacity to tolerate and go beyond disappointment and frustration.

Our own educational program, geared to younger children, was influenced by this developmental-interaction approach both in respect to educational philosophy and in the use of systematic observation of children in carrying out the program. Facilitating the child's coping and adaptation through experiences of learning and of play was emphasized. Many specific examples have been described in *The Challenge of Daycare*. For example, in noting the influence of the principle of providing the child with opportunities to act upon his environment, we said:

> . . . this . . . influences program planning in many ways, ranging from providing opportunities that allow the child to act according to his preferences of a given moment, to planning quite detailed experiences that are meant to involve specific intellectual, social, emotional, or motoric activity. At a particular time, for example, a space might be arranged in which a child could creep about the floor practicing the skill while going toward whatever object or person might look attractive to him; a child might be helped to say a word clearly or to complete a puzzle or to seek his way through a problem; he might be helped to make connections between body language and spoken language or thought, to say he is afraid or sad or happy, or make a social overture to another child. Responsive people who value the child stimulate increased competence. They help him invest physical and mental energy in the kinds of skills, communication, expression of feelings, and ways of coping that are especially useful to his developmental progress. The ability to be active in relation to his external world influences and is closely related to his increasingly complex internal world of thought and feeling.

Gradually he comes to learn that he has choices to make, options to exercise, activities to initiate; he realizes that not only the powerful adult, but he, too, can choose and influence the environment of which he is a part. Some things he must be taught or told; many other he must be allowed to discover for himself. [P. 83]

In this chapter we have tried to describe the major influences on the clinical and educational practices that characterized our program. Our strong preference was to include in our clinical awareness all the significant factors that converge and interact rather than to rule out one or more of them. In stating our preference for embracing complexity and struggling with it, we are fully aware that we will be criticized for "contaminating" the field of observation and action. Our preference reflects two factors: that in action research, as indicated earlier, the investigators are necessarily part of the field of observation and must be taken into account in understanding the data; and, second, that consideration of the multiple factors that influence development and of their interaction strikes us as important for both research and clinical practice. This position is congenial with one recently described by Sander (1980): "Research in the area of early development is currently experiencing a transition in emphasis from the classical experimental approach, which aims at isolating variables, reducing sources of variability and pursuing a linear concept of causality, toward the study of concurrent and interactive effects of multiple variables, mechanisms of integration, and the formulation of nonlinear concepts of causality. [It] . . . is looking toward biological models and methods of investigating living processes from the holistic, evolutionary and systems perspectives of biology" (p. 178). Sander argues persuasively that such research is badly needed for enrichment of the empirical base of prospective data from which a more astute conceptualization of the developmental process can be constructed.

We agree with Sander that the increasing assumption of responsibility by clinical facilities to intervene actively at the earliest pre- and postnatal periods in order to prevent or alleviate developmental deviations when either the infant or the caregiving environment is considered at risk for such deviations underscores the need for people in the child-care field to grapple with the difficult tasks of multivariate, interactive factors and to embrace complex rather than simplified theoretical approaches.

In diagnosis and in treatment, clinicians assign high relevance to some data and less to others on the basis of a view of their explanatory power and their usefulness in guiding treatment. Clinical constructs are best developed by linking theory closely to empirical findings. More specifically, the interaction of clinical data and theoretical assumptions and the examination of one against the other provide important guidelines for practice. This is an open system that is influenced in a continuing way by new discoveries—some reflecting progress, others, temporarily impeding it.

PART II   CASE REPORTS

The five families presented in the case examples were selected from the seventeen studied for several reasons. They represent the range of health and pathology, of strengths and problems, of need and capacity for change, of need but limited capacity for change—all found within the so-called culture of poverty. These five examples also illustrate the variety of family patterns represented in the study.

The first case, that of Miss Galer and Steven, places more emphasis than the other cases do on illustrating in detail how the work was done by the social worker, pediatrician, developmental examiner, and teacher in contact with the mother and child and on the way in which staff worked together to facilitate the intervention. Though the same methods and services applied to the other cases also, in them we have chosen to emphasize other dimensions of the experience. The names of the families have been changed as well as other identifying information, but care has been taken to preserve the psychological integrity of each case.

In order to simplify communication we have designated initials for the pediatrician, social worker, teacher, and developmental examiner as though only four persons were involved. In fact, each initial stands for several staff members. Our designations Dr. P. (pediatrician), Dr. D. (developmental examiner), Mrs. S. (social worker), Miss T. (teacher-nurse-caregiver) include all professionals and paraprofessionals in their functional roles. When no specific child is referred to we have used the masculine pronoun to avoid the awkwardness of she/he, her/him designation. Similarly the parent is "she" unless a father is specified. We trust that the reader will recognize this as a convenience.

CHAPTER 4

Motivation and Courage:
Overcoming Poverty
Miss Galer and Steven

Miss Galer, 17 when she became pregnant, was the fifth of seven children in an inner-city black family headed by her mother. Her father had left the family when Miss Galer was 8 years old. She did not know where he was but had been told he was a drug addict. As far back as Miss Galer could remember the family had been on welfare, though her mother now had a part-time job in a factory. As a young adolescent Miss Galer had experienced being on welfare as a humiliation. Having to apply for AFDC for herself during her pregnancy aroused very angry feelings which focused on her impression that the welfare worker assumed she would want to place her baby in adoption. This experience stirred up memories of a time when, on the basis of what she described as false reports, her mother had been called neglectful and threatened with removal of the children.

Miss Galer's motivation for joining the study was undoubtedly related in part to her wish to escape from welfare into financial independence. She felt poorly prepared to do so. Although she had a high school diploma, she said she had learned little. Her last year had been extremely turbulent because racial tension and riots in her school had created fear and unrest. During the last months of high school she had also been upset about being pregnant. Miss Galer appeared to be an intelligent young woman but one who was educationally as well as socioeconomically deprived.

Because she was distressed and embarrassed about being pregnant, Miss Galer sought no medical care until the seventh month of pregnancy. But from that point on she had good obstetrical care. The infant, named Steven, was born at term. The father, who was the same age as Miss Galer, visited her and the baby in the hospital.

He had been invited to be part of the process by which parents joined the study, but he took no part beyond conveying through Miss Galer his approval of her participation. We were never to have more than a brief glimpse of him during one of his hospital visits. Miss Galer told us that he had offered marriage, but she had not accepted because she was unsure of her feeling for him. Much later she added that her mother had opposed the marriage since it would have meant that her daughter and grandchild would live with the paternal grandparents.

The pediatrician Steven was to have all through the project, Dr. P., observed and examined him twenty minutes after delivery and found him to be a normal newborn. Dr. P. and the social worker, Mrs. S., were already known to Miss Galer; each had had several interviews with her during the month preceding delivery. Each according to plan visited her on the day of delivery. To Mrs. S. she spoke of how much it had helped when she was admitted to the hospital to have had the antepartum orientation visit to the obstetrical floor that we had arranged for her. She was feeling very reassured also by Dr. P.'s prompt examination of the baby. She thought our interest in her had caused the hospital staff to be especially helpful. When the baby was brought to her from the newborn nursery, she described the awe she felt and her surprise about what he could already do.

Dr. P. saw Steven for a discharge examination on the third postpartum day and visited him at home a week later. Though Miss Galer had not requested the visit, she asked several questions about matters of mild concern and reported details which caused Dr. P. to suggest giving the baby a stronger formula. She mentioned the date of the next pediatric examination, three weeks hence, but also stressed her availability whenever Miss Galer might have questions or concerns.

Home for Miss Galer and Steven was with her mother, two sisters, and four brothers. The grandmother's presence during the early home visits of both the pediatrician and the social worker gave us our first intimation that Miss Galer might have difficulty assuming and maintaining the role of mother to her child. The maternal grandmother as an experienced mother was providing most of the care for Steven and was allowing Miss Galer to remain an observer of the bathing, dressing, and feeding. She was still the major care-giver when Mrs. S. visited Miss Galer three weeks after Steven's birth.

Soon, however, Miss Galer began to impress us as well motivated to learn about child care from both her mother and the study staff and able to ask good questions about physical care and aspects of development, such as how a baby learns to talk. She spoke of want-ing to be a good mother to Steven, to be the person to whom he was most attached. By the time Steven was a month old, Miss Galer had assumed full care of him. She decided not to go to school or work. That would have to come later because she wanted to take care of Steven herself.

A Life-threatening Illness

At 6 weeks of age, in spite of good care, Steven developed a near-fatal respiratory infection, culminating in the need for a tracheos-tomy. His pediatrician, in response to Miss Galer's telephone call, saw Steven at home, found him much sicker than he had been when she had examined him the day before, and took him and his mother to the hospital, where he was admitted to the intensive care unit. During his hospitalization over a period of eight weeks Dr. P. was in daily contact with the hospital staff and with Steven. Both Dr. P. and Mrs. S. saw Miss Galer at regular intervals also, answering her questions and trying to be supportive. She was especially concerned that her own respiratory infection predating Steven's had been the cause of his illness, and she was worried that something unusual might be wrong with him that caused him to become so ill. She was spending many hours a day at the hospital, became over-fatigued and was frequently near tears. At this time being supportive in-cluded something as simple and basic as finding out that Miss Galer hadn't eaten all day and insisting on continuing the conversation over food in the hospital cafeteria.

When Steven was a little better Miss Galer began to think about the effect of the illness and the tracheostomy on him. Here she drew on an earlier discussion of how children learn to talk. She was receptive to the idea that Steven might have trouble making the usual baby sounds, so it would be important to continue talking to him even without any vocal stimulation or response from him. She acknowledged being aware that before his illness she had talked to him a lot but had stopped, almost as if she thought he couldn't hear her because he did not make sounds.

When Steven had recovered sufficiently to permit it, he had his first developmental examination at 14 weeks while still in the hospital. Dr. D., the developmental examiner, found that he was delayed in motor development and, of course, early language, presumably because of his illness. He had difficulty making any sounds because of the tube in his throat and was restricted in motion because of the need to hyperextend his neck for easier breathing.

When it was determined that the tracheostomy tube would need to be continued after Steven's discharge from the hospital, Miss Galer was taught how to use the necessary equipment, how to remove, clean, and reinsert the tube, and how to keep Steven comfortable with the help of a misting machine. She learned to do all of this competently and spent several nights in his hospital room to assure herself that if he became distressed in breathing during the night she would awaken.

Before Steven's discharge Miss Galer moved to her own apartment at some distance from her mother. Although she was concerned that her mother would "feel hurt" she said she did it to protect Steven, so that he could be where no one smoked and she could control the temperature and thus make it easier for him to breathe. We were not expecting this show of independence in view of Miss Galer's initial reliance on her mother's care of Steven. We speculated, however, that the psychological support and medical care we supplied, together with her wish to be "the most important person to Steven," prompted her move.

During the period just before and after Steven's discharge, Dr. P. and Mrs. S. helped her get special equipment for his care and helped with transportation to the hospital for weekly after-care visits, sometimes combining these trips with stops for grocery shopping and other errands that were difficult for her during Steven's convalescence. Such trips began or ended with time for discussion of whatever she felt pressure to talk about. Family team members were especially concerned about the vigilance necessary for Steven's safety, vigilance which she was demonstrating but which we felt would be very exhausting for her. In our staff discussions at this time we were especially concerned that Miss Galer had moved away from home and the help of her mother and younger adolescent sisters just when it was especially needed. However, after a brief period of alienation between Miss Galer and her mother, family members did visit and offer help. The problem became rather one of Miss Galer's not feeling safe if she left Steven in anyone else's care even briefly. Offers of a few hours of care at Children's House to relieve her and allow her freedom for errands were not accepted at this time. However, two months after Steven's discharge she was not only continuing to provide good care but showing considerable capacity to enjoy him. She continued to be thoughtful about his development and to want to talk over questions such as what affect the tracheostomy tube would have on him as he got older, how he would feel about himself, and how other children would react to him. She had also begun thinking about Steven's need for a father later on, but expressed concern over feeling unwilling to share him. Meanwhile, the father had moved to another community, and Miss Galer rarely mentioned him.

From Happy Reciprocity to Signs of Stress

When Steven was almost 6 months old, Mrs. S. observed that Miss Galer's care of him was very sensitive, considerate, and skillful, that there was an unusual amount of visual communication between them, that Steven's face was very expressive, that his mother was indeed talking to him, and that as had been suggested to her she was imitating his mouth movements and adding what seemed to be appropriate sounds, much to his delight. It was also observed that there was an adequate supply of appropriate toys, including toys which would allow him to produce sounds, another thing that had been suggested to his mother. At times she held him comfortably against her body, at other times sat him on her lap facing her. Each watched the other intently. Much of their play together took place in this way, with mutual smiling and with Miss Galer supplying vocalization for Steven's mouth movements and stimulating his imitation of her mouth movements when she spoke to him. Their delight in each other was striking. Both mother and infant seemed content to enjoy the holding, looking, "mugging," talking, and smiling that were their main social interaction. What was lacking, however, was any attempt on the mother's part to help Steven become interested in toys. Even so he passed his six-month developmental examination with Dr. D. well above age level, having overcome the problem of his motor skills seen earlier. His language could still not be appraised but his ability to convey affective states was such that he was considered quite responsive socially. In fact, both in the developmental evaluation situation and elsewhere he was noted to establish social contact with his mother and others through his facial expressions and visual searching.

It was not until the seventh month that we saw some of the effects on Miss Galer of having devoted herself so exclusively to Steven's care and allowing herself so few distractions and little enjoyment aside from her enjoyment of him. It was during the monthly pediatric exam with Dr. P. that some of her discouragement with the relentless daily routine came out. For the first time she expressed worry that her having to change Steven's tube would cause him to connect pain with her and to like other people better. Contributing to her mood was the fact that a welfare check stolen three weeks earlier had not yet been replaced in spite of calls to both the welfare office and legal aid. The social worker's offer to intervene produced prompt action, and when she visited Miss Galer a week later she found her in a much lighter mood. Nevertheless, the intense enjoyment of each other seen earlier in Miss Galer and Steven was no longer visible. Steven didn't appear distressed but neither did he seem enchanted with his mother as he had earlier. For the first time since shortly after Steven's birth Miss Galer spoke of wanting to support Steven and herself and wanting to use some of the time at home to study in preparation for later training. The timing suggested that she was understandably looking forward to diversion from child care. Further discussion of what she needed to study and acknowledgment that she had tried unsuccessfully to study by herself led to an offer, which she readily accepted, of a Yale student volunteer as a tutor.

Aside from her oblique reference to wanting something for herself, some distraction from Steven's care, Miss Galer seemed to want to avoid discussing with her social worker the discontent she had expressed to Dr. P.; instead, she kept a lively discussion of other subjects going. However, Mrs. S. found an opportunity to refer to her concern that Steven would connect pain with her. In the discussion that followed no attempt was made to call attention to the change in the emotional communication between Steven and her or to associate the lessened enjoyment between them with her discontent. Instead, Mrs. S. lightly touched upon the desirability of her having some pleasurable diversions from his care. She also suggested that it was important to offset any pain she felt he associated with her through pleasurable experiences. She further suggested that pleasure was available to him in the kinds of social play they both enjoyed and that another source could be provided by helping him to enjoy toys. How this might be done was demonstrated directly with Steven.

Later during that visit Miss Galer asked whether or not she should be helping Steven learn to walk, perhaps reflecting a wish now for him to grow up. When some of the precursors of walking were mentioned to her, she said she would have to get over her reluctance to have him on the floor, where he could get dirty. Stimulating Steven's crawling by putting an interesting toy slightly out of his reach and providing opportunities for him to pull to a standing position were discussed with her as ways of promoting skills that would lead to walking in five or six months. As the visit ended Mrs. S. spoke again about arranging for a tutor and offered to lend Miss Galer some books in which she had expressed interest.

When Steven was 8 months old his father appeared asking to see him. Miss Galer allowed this but thereafter spent an entire interview with Mrs. S. at Children's House discussing her ambivalence about the father's showing up. Through the discussion she decided her concern was that Steven's father would not be a reliable person in his life but would let him down as she felt he had let her down. That this concern was probably also related to her father's disappearance from her life was not suggested to her by Mrs. S., but this insight contributed to our understanding of some of Miss Galer's behavior and attitudes.

Steven was 9 months old before Miss Galer talked with Mrs. S. about her difficulty in letting anyone else care for him. Mrs. S. responded to her rationalization about fearing to endanger him by reminding her of her inability to leave him even briefly at Children's House, where both pediatric and nursing care were available. She acknowledged then that the real reason had to be something else. After thinking for a moment or two she said she thought she was too guilty to use that help. Mrs. S. responded that, yes, she had been behaving as if she had to do penance. Miss Galer laughed and agreed it was like that. At this point she did not seem ready to discuss the reasons for her guilt, and it was felt that this was something she would think about and discuss later. Mrs. S.'s impression was that the interview had provided an opportunity for Miss Galer to develop more insight about her own behavior than she was yet ready to recognize with Mrs. S. but that even without such discussion her behavior might change. This was almost immediately confirmed when she spoke of her determination to have some relief from taking care of Steven. She added that she hadn't really resented him yet, but she might. Thereafter Miss Galer began allowing her sister to care for Steven for brief periods.

Miss Galer's relatively depressed mood related to her isolation and the months of vigilance and special care required by Steven were reflected in his performance on the developmental examination at 9 months. It was noted by Dr. D. that he was doing less well in all areas of development than he had done at 6 months—i.e., in motor development, performance with the test materials, speech, and social development. While differentiation and developmental progress were occurring in some respects at a normal rate, Dr. D. noted less good integration of behavior and dampening of Steven's earlier delightful affective expressiveness. He was more sober than before and he looked often at his mother somewhat anxiously. He was responsive to social contact but did not initiate it. His preoccupation with mouthing and banging the toys inhibited his using them in other ways, although at times he had flashes of investigatory interest and selective preference for some toys over others. We were not worried about his basic intelligence or about the strength of the attachment between mother and child. We felt, however, that his performance reflected increased stress in his daily life. While some aspects of his performance no doubt could be understood as an increasingly perceptive infant's reactions to his tracheostomy and the medical procedures connected with it, the greatest change in his daily experience was his mother's more frequent depressed mood. While continuing to be very conscientious about his care and concerned for him, she was less in tune with him than she had been earlier. It appeared, too, that she had probably not been able to respond to the suggestion of using toys in her interaction with Steven and that his experience in play with objects was very limited. It was striking that Miss Galer asked almost no questions of Dr. D. about the results of the testing though observers felt she was aware that Steven was not responding as expected to the tasks involving toys.

During the next home visit Mrs. S. waited to see whether Miss Galer would bring up any concern about the developmental examination. She did do so and asked for suggestions as to how to help him. Some specific suggestions were made, including that *she* play at putting small bright objects like blocks or poker chips into a bottle, cup, or pan, dumping them out and putting them in again, then handing the block or chip to Steven, inviting him to imitate. Playing pat-a-cake and trying to get him to imitate that were also suggested. In accordance with a tendency noted earlier to be interested in the how and why of things, Miss Galer asked why imitation was important, thus providing an opportunity to help her understand its value not only at the time but in his ongoing development.

During these months of Steven's first year, Miss Galer was continuing to use Dr. P. well, to ask good questions during pediatric exams, and to use good judgment about telephoning when she was worried about Steven. She was becoming a good observer of her child and feeling more assurance about her mothering. That she could complain a bit about being burdened suggested that she was feeling easier about his survival. She sometimes discussed nonmedical matters with both Dr. P. and Mrs. S. but never in a way that suggested she was checking to see if they would contradict one another. She seemed comfortable and even reassured that they and Dr. D. also were in close touch about anything concerning her welfare and Steven's.

During an interview when Steven was 11 months, Miss Galer brought up her fear that a younger sister might imitate her by becoming pregnant. This opened up discussion of why she thought *she* had become pregnant when she had obviously had other plans for herself. It is not important here to present the details but over time it was possible, using information that she had given at intervals, to help her understand her own behavior as she had not done before. That it had been neurotically overdetermined was evident, and eventually it was possible for her to understand more fully the connection between her guilt about the pregnancy and her earlier inability to accept any relief from the arduousness of Steven's care.

Problems and Solutions

At the 12-month developmental examination Dr. D. found Steven a little delayed in all but his social development. However, he was delightfully responsive, though clearly more so to his mother than to Dr. D. He was trusting of relatively strange adults and quite charming. His way of interacting in the developmental exam situation, seldom through the medium of a toy, was of course reflective of his mother's style of play with him and handicapped him in doing a number of test items. In considering after the evaluation how to help Steven overcome his delays in development, we concluded that his mother would not be able to help him in the particular way necessary, for reasons about which we could only speculate. We decided to suggest that he start toddler school as soon as possible.

In the next interview with Mrs. S., Miss Galer again expressed concern about Steven's not doing what Dr. D. expected with the toys. She spoke of her discouragement that when she tried to use toys with him he wanted to just bang with them or sweep them away. Her concern gave Mrs. S. the opportunity to say that children sometimes needed help in learning to play, that that was one purpose of toddler school. Miss Galer was enthusiastic about this possibility for him to be helped and it was agreed that he could start at age 15 months. It should be recalled that toddler school was held for one and a half hours twice each week with mothers present.

Fortunately it was possible for the surgeon to remove Steven's tracheostomy tube shortly before he entered toddler school. However, both before and after its removal he was vulnerable to respiratory infections and his condition required vigilance from his mother and quick response from Dr. P. at all hours of the day and night. Steven's starting toddler school seemed to stimulate Miss Galer to think more specifically about plans for her future, and with Mrs. S. she began to explore possibilities for training, eventually deciding that she would like to become a physiotherapy aide. She asked Mrs. S. to help her find out about training opportunities. The following is quoted from an interview that took place shortly after her request. It illustrates some aspects of Miss Galer's personality and some aspects of our role with study mothers:

Miss Galer complained of not sleeping well. Exploration of possible reasons resulted in her thinking of several but the one she wanted to focus on was sexual tension resulting from abstention. She spoke of thinking it wasn't right to have sex outside of marriage. She said she would worry, too, about pregnancy: she thought "the pill" dangerous and wasn't sure other things worked. I suggested that she could talk this over with the gynecologist she was seeing but added that perhaps she was more concerned about sex for her not being, as she said, right. She spoke then of having some continuing guilt about being an unmarried mother. In spite of all the talk about the new sexual freedom and all the "braving it out" involved in girls keeping their babies, she said, having a child when unmarried was still not acceptable, not to her or to others. She continued, saying she was surprised at her mother's not having disapproved of her pregnancy. I asked if she had wanted her mother to do so. When she said she thought so, I asked if she had wanted me to. She agreed but said she had learned I didn't judge her or try to tell her what to do but helped her think out what was right for her. Miss G. referred to having had intercourse several times with Tom since Steven's birth, saying he was an old friend she had gone with before she knew Steven's father. She hinted that this meant she was promiscuous. I suggested that for her as a healthy young woman at an age when sexual feelings were strong to have had two sequential sexual experiences within sustained relationships did not mean to me that she was promiscuous, but what was important was what it meant to her. She relaxed visibly and there was a pause while she seemed to be thinking over our conversation. Then she referred to plans for training. I asked if during her silence she had made a connection between having a sexual experience with Tom and her wish to get some training. She said, "That's right. It doesn't make any sense for you to be helping me to have more education if I'm going to get pregnant and not be able to use it." During the rest of the hour we covered the following: that I was helping her to find out about educational opportunities because she had asked me to, but that she could at any time ask me not to; that my role was to help her know what options were available; that together we could explore where various choices would take her, what the advantages and disadvantages of each might be for her at this time in her life; that I did not make choices for her but would help her all I could with her chosen goals.

Shortly after the above interview, Miss Galer, acting on information given her, applied for and with the help of letters of reference from Dr. P. and Mrs. S. was accepted for training as a physiotherapy aide. She was relieved and pleased, but as the time to begin her training drew near, she felt highly ambivalent about not being able to care for Steven herself. Recurrence of the concern that she might not be the most important person to Steven appeared to be related not to Steven's enjoyment of his relationship to the toddler school staff but to Miss Galer's mother. At about this time she and Steven had moved back to her mother's house temporarily in order to help with the illness of a family member. Soon she reported a recurrent fear, apparent earlier but now more openly expressed, that her mother was taking over with Steven. He was beginning to go to his grand- mother—not to her—when he wanted something. The result of a long and circuitous interview was that she began to see that while Steven's grandmother did, indeed, like to mother him, Miss Galer had allowed it to happen by acting not like an adult and the mother of her own child but, once back in her mother's house, like the girl she had been before Steven's birth.

The interview was typical of many in which Miss Galer brought up a problem and could be helped to think about not only other people's contributing motives and behavior but her own, with re- sulting insight and relief. Such use of interviews was possible, of course, only as she felt respected and valued. Then she could tolerate seeing her part in creating a problem. Her reward was ability to reduce or resolve tension or conflict by means of changes in her own behavior without expecting others to change theirs.

At Steven's 18-month developmental evaluation, three months after he started toddler school, Dr. D. found his overall development im- proved, and he scored somewhat above age level on the test items. His progress in language was especially noteworthy. Observers com- mented on his very special relationship with his mother, his sharing of pleasure with her. This special relationship was both a delight to see and the basis of Steven's difficulty in adjusting to full daycare, which was started eight weeks later, when he was 20 months, be- cause his mother began her training program.

Daycare and the Pain of Separation

Preparation of the daycare staff to receive Steven included the pre- diction that he would have a more than usually difficult time adjust- ing to separation from his mother and that his ways of reacting might not be easily identified as a separation problem. Miss Galer cooperated in preparing Steven for daycare by spending time with him at the center during the first days. While his mother was present, the experience for him was like being with her in toddler school, and he did well. It was when the time came for him to be without her, not for a short time but for the whole day, that the stress he experienced was greatly increased. Though there were isolated instances when his play and behavior suggested some interest and even pleasure in his activities, he asked over and over for help with things he was fully capable of doing, became unusually tired and sleepy, and needed comfort early in the day. This he sought by asking to have what we regarded as his transitional object, a pacifier with a scarf belonging to his mother tied through the ring. During the first week an observer recorded: "Steven was tired and upset well before lunchtime and began to demand his pacifier. When it was given to him, he sucked it madly as though it was the only comfort he had in the world." Sometimes he didn't put the pacifier in his mouth but held the scarf against his cheek. On some days he clutched it most of the time, which made it impossible for him to take part in certain activities.

From his toddler school experience Steven knew a number of the daycare staff, including Miss T., who was now his special caregiver-teacher. We became concerned as he continued to turn not to her or to other familiar staff when in need but to his pacifier, though if he had the pacifier first he would sometimes accept an offered lap. We discussed Steven's behavior and agreed that unless he could be helped to trust his caregiver, not only would he profit much less from the program in terms of the development of skills but daycare would be a psychologically painful experience for him. Shortening his day at the center, which would have been our choice, was not possible for his mother to arrange. We were concerned about what it was costing this child to try to cope with the separation, but at home he gave his mother no reason to question the daycare plan. She reported enthusiastically how much he was learning and how well he seemed to have adjusted.

Our concern increased when after a month Steven was still making little progress in coming to rely on his special caregiver. He seemed usually to seek response from the least familiar person in the room. He behaved at times in an independent, pseudomature way, smiling at and relating superficially to all staff. This behavior was then extended to visitors, with Steven behaving as the official greeter. We asked his mother again to spend some time with him at the center, but she was able to do so only once. The result was Steven's increased reliance on Miss T., but only for a very short time. We considered the possibility that his mother was reluctant to have him become at all attached to one person, but there was no evidence of this. When our concern was discussed with her, she seemed to understand very well why so young a child away from his mother needed the comfort and safety of a substitute for her, of a person who would know him especially well. She had been aware that this was our plan for every child before she entered Steven in daycare and seemed accepting of it then and later.

Complicating the problem of helping Steven cope with separation was that as he turned to observers and visitors for attention, Miss T. began to feel unsuccessful and to doubt Steven's capacity for anything but a superficial relationship. She felt he wasn't using what the program offered and wasn't learning. She was right in that he was not able to make full use of the program; yet four months after he entered, the 24-month developmental evaluation showed that he had made nine months' progress in six months, with the biggest gains in the important areas of language skills and problem solving, an indication that cognitive development was proceeding even though the separation problem was still very active. These findings, however, did little to reassure his teacher. She was only a little comforted by being reminded that a separation problem had been predicted for Steven and that he was expressing it in behavior that said, in effect, "If I can't have my mother, anyone will do."

Improving the Staff's Effectiveness

Miss T. was not alone in her reaction to Steven. For a time most of the daycare staff was put off by his tending to flit from one person to another with no tie deepening. Without conscious intent, some withdrawal of interest in Steven occurred to which he reacted with still more activity toward peripheral people. Because sensitive and devoted care of very young children is extremely difficult to provide day after day, there must be some gratification in the form of favorable response to effort. If that is lacking, there must be strong staff support from program leaders. Otherwise morale and ultimately the program suffer. Such support was given; problem-solving meetings were held to help everyone understand more clearly the reasons for the separation problem, its particular manifestation in Steven, and the pain that was partly covered by his smiling, affable bids for response from visitors. Attention was called to the staff's relative withdrawal from Steven, and the necessity for correcting it was stressed.

The discussion had the effect of recathecting the child. Suggestions were made for ways of helping him cope. Miss T. was asked to spent some part of each day with Steven alone doing something he enjoyed. She was also asked to take a photograph of him and his mother that would be his to keep at the center. Steven's response to his special time with his teacher was gratifying. Concerning his reaction to the photograph, a staff member recorded: "When it was given to Steven, he was almost overwhelmed with emotion. He trembled, talked to it, hugged it to his chest, and patted it. He almost cried. He kept it under his plate at lunch and took it to his cot for nap. It was emotion packed, almost a living thing for him. Many times he said, 'My momma, *my* momma.'" Steven continued to keep the photograph near him throughout his time in daycare.

As all staff, but Miss T. in particular, renewed interest in and effort with Steven, his initial tendency to act helpless, to become overly fatigued, to need responses from visitors lessened. There was still evidence that being in daycare was stressful for him, but it was manifested in behavior that helped him to cope better. For example, he played often at games involving separation and reunion, and much of his talk each day was about the car that took him home at day's end.

Training for Employment:
Mother and Child See It Through

Part of Steven's burden during his ten months in daycare was that his home life was considerably less gratifying than it had been before his mother began her training. She was at school long hours, had to study at night, and could spend only an hour or so with him in the evening. She reported that he was more irritable, had begun to be a little aggressive, hitting, scratching, and spitting when he felt deprived, was demanding of her attention, and was exploiting her continuing anxiety about his breathing. He had learned to cough and act as if he couldn't breathe when he wanted to distract her from her studying. He also began being reluctant to go to bed in order to have time with her. Until they learned this, the daycare staff had been puzzled about why he was exhibiting signs of real sleep deficit, not the tendency to quick fatigue seen earlier.

Miss Galer's full day in her training course meant that it was impossible to continue contact with Dr. P. and Mrs. S. in person, though she stayed out of school if Steven was ill or was scheduled for a pediatric or developmental examination. She kept in touch with both Dr. P. and Mrs. S. by telephone in the evening, sometimes asking for help with school assignments, sometimes wanting to talk about problems with her mother or siblings or about how to handle some new facet of Steven's behavior. These telephone conversations also served to provide liaison between home and daycare. At times this involved letting Steven's mother know about trips and outings and special events so that she could be receptive to his talk about them at home. Sometimes the focus was on coordinating home and daycare toilet training, sometimes simply letting Miss Galer know what Steven was doing in daycare or clarifying for her some information he had reported.

In spite of stress and fatigue related to her own arduous schedule, Miss Galer was pleased with Steven's development, continued to speak of how much he was gaining from daycare, and was especially pleased about his increasing vocabulary, his interest in books, his ability to tell her about his experiences and to communicate his feelings. While what she called his beginning to have a mind of his own sometimes made life harder for her, she was proud of his assertiveness. When he tried to focus her attention on him by doing something that would concern her, like the coughing and heavy breathing, she dealt with his behavior appropriately but described enjoyment of his cleverness.

Miss Galer's early concern about sharing Steven with his father was no longer heard and was never evident in her relationship to Children's House staff. When Steven was 2 she again allowed his father to visit him, but as expected he made no plan for future contact. Because of her references to difficulty sharing Steven, we had wondered whether she would be able to allow him optimal autonomy. Perhaps her concern about sharing was more tied up than she knew with the responsibility she felt to be vigilant about his health, and as his health improved and fewer crises occurred, she could relax. In any case, when he began to exhibit 2-year-old assertiveness and independence, there were the usual confrontations over what she wisely could not allow him to do, but there was no indication of wishing to suppress his independence and initiative.

Reaching Two-Year-Old Competence

During the last six months of the study, in spite of still missing his mother, Steven was able to make good use of the daycare program and to grow in social, emotional, and cognitive development in ways that were evident *in* the program, not just in developmental evaluation, thus reassuring and rewarding his caregivers. His relationships to other children and adults lost their superficial quality and reflected instead the give and take typical of young children. Some examples follow of quite mature ability to share with others, to engage in cooperative play, to learn, to enjoy creative activity with peers, and to be a special "friend."

At 25 months: Steven arrived this morning with a chocolate bar at which he had been nibbling. As soon as he was in the door he went to Jackie and stuck in it his mouth, watching closely until Jackie got a bite. Then he went to Larry and did the same thing. As soon as his coat and hat were off, he took a bite and repeated the procedure. All of this was done with excited, happy talking. It was as if Steven was delighted to have the candy to share. Later in the morning Steven and Jackie with Miss T's encouragement began building a tower with large blocks. They took turns adding blocks. Soon it became too high to reach. Jackie got a chair, stood on it, and Steven handed him more blocks, enabling them to build it even higher.

At 26 months: When the teacher drew a picture of Steven at his request, he could name and point to his own and the picture's eyes, ears, nose, mouth, neck, shoulders, arms, fingers, hands, legs, feet, and ankles, indicating both cognitive growth and the development of a clear sense of his own body.

At 28 months: Steven, Curtis and Jackie were playing instruments, Steven banging the drum, Curtis shaking the tambourine, and Jackie the cymbals. They were obviously making music together, watching and smiling at one another. Curtis and Jackie stopped playing after a bit, and Steven pointed at them with his drumstick saying the equivalent of, "Come on and play, you guys." Curtis and Jackie joined in again. Curtis and Steven both bobbed rhythmically as they played, and each also occasionally exclaimed something as they played—vocal accompaniment? Later that day when Jackie cried, Steven offered him the car he had brought in the morning. On Miss T.'s lap Jackie accepted Steven's car but continued to cry. Steven wiped away Jackie's tears and said, "Don't cry." Then he patted his back and said, "All right now."

At 29 months: Jackie wanted Steven to play with him when Steven was otherwise engaged. He refused and Jackie became quite upset. In what appeared to be a placating and apologetic mood, Steven went to Jackie, hugged him and kissed him on the cheek, then went back to his own play.

These examples illustrate mature behaviors that came about spontaneously in Steven and other children, partly, we believe, because of their experiences in daycare but without staff asking these things of them. Steven's concern for Jackie's feelings is but one of many recorded examples of a child looking after another's welfare.

Steven's close relationship to his mother during the first 20 months of life contributed both to his separation problem and to his ability to respond to special efforts to help him. That separation remained something of a problem, however, is illustrated by the fact that the longest sentence he was ever heard to utter came very near the end of the study when he said, "After nap Uncle John come in his car—take me home to Mommy." That distress over separation did not have a serious effect on Steven's learning was borne out by his final developmental evaluation at 30 months. He had some successes as high as 36 and 42 months and a solid overall score in the average range.

Two months before the end of the project Steven's mother accepted a job which she was to begin three months later, on completing her training. The emphasis in the last period of our work with her was on planning for Steven's care when Children's House closed. While she was distressed about losing daycare for Steven, her school work was now less draining and her goal of becoming self-supporting was in sight. She was pleased that she would soon be able to pay for Steven's private medical care with a pediatrician Dr. P. would recommend.

Follow-up

Five years after the close of Children's House, the families were seen in the follow-up studies mentioned earlier. When Miss Galer was interviewed she could think of nothing about 7½-year-old Steven that displeased her: "He has a good personality and is good company. He still uses a lot of nonverbal ways of communicating, especially to show affection. He has been a rather quiet child, doing more thinking than talking, and until recently an indoor book-loving child, but now he is growing more fond of outdoor activities. He is doing well in school and is popular with other children." She added that his only trouble at school was during the first year, when the exploring and questioning he learned at Children's House upset his teacher. His mother had then arranged for Steven to go to school outside the neighborhood because in her opinion the inner-city public school available to him would not provide the kind of education she wanted him to have. Her report, as well as the scores on the Peabody Individual Achievement Test, revealed that his academic performance was good.

When Steven was seen by a psychologist not on the project staff as part of the follow-up, it was learned on testing that he had maintained his solid average development. However, more impressive were certain aspects of his personality. Excerpts from the psychologist's report follow:

> He gives the impression of having significant self-esteem and a sense of his own integrity. The animation of his facial expression is noteworthy for its richness. A range of affect is observed from scowling dismay with difficulty to grinning, animated pleasure and comfortable joking; he gives the impression of a happy, easygoing, and spontaneous child. A most charming and delightful child with whom to work, Steven is immediately warm and direct in his interaction with the examiner. Throughout the testing he is responsive to the examiner's input, both her demands and her support, and he actively seeks help from her when needed. When he disagrees with the examiner . . . he is able to state his point and support his argument comfortably. He interacts warmly with his mother, as she does with him, and one observes a mutually caring and supportive relationship. Steven's mother shows pleasure when he teases and jokes with the examiner as well as when he teases her. Steven turns to her frequently during the testing to share a smile, or to get a nod of reassurance, and she responds warmly at such times. Most salient about Steven is his warmth and funloving spontaneity which make a testing situation an enjoyable experience without significantly interfering with his problem solving.

At follow-up Miss Galer had supported herself and her son for five years. With child care and a training program made possible through the project, she had achieved a goal of great importance to her. As Steven's sound development testifies, she had done so without jeopardizing her child's future.

CHAPTER 5

Lost in the Woods:
Seeking a Way Out
Mrs. Ives and Carrie

When we first knew Mrs. Ives, then aged 20, she had lived for ten months in a common-law relationship with Mr. Ives, the father of the baby about to be born. Mrs. Ives was the first of eight children in a marginally functioning white family often supported by public welfare, a family that on at least one occasion had moved out of state to prevent placement of some of the children. She felt that she had never, either as a child or young adult, had the support she needed from her mother. She remembered being beaten by her parents and felt herself to be the child her parents disliked the most. She had dropped out of school at age 16 after completing ninth grade and worked at various unskilled jobs. At age 19 Mrs. Ives had had a psychiatric hospitalization, with a diagnosis of acute and chronic schizophrenic reaction. Because of her thought disorder and confused memory, we learned little else of her history. Very early in our contact with her it was apparent that she had marked dependency needs and a high degree of anxiety. Although her dependency needs were met partly by project staff and sporadically by Mr. Ives, she was subject to extreme stress reactions as a result of the ordinary vicissitudes of daily life. At times of particularly high anxiety, not only was her thinking disordered but her ability to function within the home deteriorated.

Mr. Ives's functioning was only a little better than that of Mrs. Ives. He, too, was the oldest child in his family and, like Mrs. Ives, had been poorly nurtured. By the time he was 6 his father had deserted, leaving his mother with five children. She remarried twice and in between marriages had numerous alliances. By the time we knew Mr. Ives at age 23 he was alienated from his mother and siblings. He had left school after finishing the eleventh grade and joined the army, from which he received a dishonorable discharge for being AWOL. He had also had several brushes with civilian law, once having been involved in an assault on one of his stepfathers.

Mrs. Ives recognized, if Mr. Ives did not, that their relationship was characterized by their need for support from one another. Because both had been deprived in significant ways neither had the inner resources for consistently supplying what the other needed. Yet as they joined the study, each had a protective attitude toward the other and both appeared to be taking the coming responsibilities of parenthood seriously. The social worker who saw them in pre-admission interviews found them rather touching in their earnestness and said, "There is something suggestive of Hansel and Gretel lost in the woods about this young couple."

Though he was ill prepared to do so, it was Mr. Ives's strong wish to earn enough money to support the family without resorting to public welfare. He had no special skills and had limited ability to function under the pressure of any but the most undemanding work. Thus he could get only poorly paid jobs and usually had to work at two in order to have even a subsistence level of income. In spite of frequently losing jobs because of troubled relationships with fellow workmen and supervisors, Mr. Ives covered what must have been a good deal of discouragement with an air of "great expectations." He was unrealistic in his view of his abilities and prospects. His defensive stance made it difficult to introduce the possibility of a training program or other means of bringing his aspirations closer to reality. Thus throughout the two and a half years of the project, he held and lost many jobs, could support the family only marginally, and eventually became resentful of trying to do so, one factor in the gradually deteriorating relationship between the parents. Mr. Ives's long hours of work on two jobs were to have a marked effect on his availability to project staff. Only in the first few weeks of our work with this family was he seen for more than a few minutes at a time. Because of the very limited nature of the contact, his relationship to those who worked closely with Mrs. Ives remained superficial. Our dependence on her view of the difficulties between them limited our helpfulness in that context as well as in problems that arose in his relationship to his child. For that reason he is referred to minimally in what follows.

After the birth of the baby, a healthy little girl named Carrie, Mrs. Ives's anxiety focused on the child's care. Even with considerable help from Mr. Ives in the early postpartum period, she experienced extreme panic when Carrie did not behave exactly as she expected. Complicating the situation was the fact that although Carrie was a tolerant baby who gave clear signals about her state and needs, Mrs. Ives could not correctly "read" the signals. Both the social worker, Mrs. S., and the pediatrician, Dr. P., made frequent regular home visits during the first weeks after Carrie's birth. Both also received many telephone calls from Mrs. Ives, sometimes several times a day in quick succession. Sometimes she was able to be calmed and comforted by their responses to her questions or complaints about the baby. But at others, eager as she seemed for answers to her numerous questions, she could not use them.

A Normal Newborn Becomes Disturbed

The first six months of Carrie's life were particularly difficult for Mrs. Ives. Her own dependency needs were so great that she could scarcely tolerate the complete dependency of an infant. Unable in her anxiety to perceive the baby's needs and feeling states, she responded in terms of her own. For Mrs. Ives it was as if Carrie were not a separate person from her mother: if she didn't like a particular food, she assumed Carrie would not either. Her concerns about Carrie centered almost entirely on eating and sleeping. As a result she tended to overfeed, to use food as her answer to any problem. If the baby slept a little longer than usual at a particular time, Mrs. Ives telephoned in fright, asking if she should try to wake her.

The natural style of both parents was to play with Carrie at times and in ways that pleased them but were often overstimulating, unrelated to the baby's needs at the moment, and at times overwhelming. Their play with her was body play, without the introduction of toys, though use of toys was frequently suggested to them and demonstrated in staff interaction with Carrie.

Although we had been concerned about this baby almost from the beginning because of the mother's high anxiety, excitability, wide mood swings, and poor sense of reality leading to inappropriate behavior with the infant, it was not until 6 months that the effects of Carrie's daily care were clearly visible in her performance on developmental evaluation and the concomitant observations of other aspects of her behavior. She had become a psychologically disturbed infant. As with many overwhelmed children, there was a marked decrease in her activity of every kind. She was subdued, relatively uninterested in the testing toys, socially much less responsive than previously; she was physically inactive and, though not ill, sleepy, or hungry, was fretful and her irritable cry reflected real distress. We could only speculate about how much more disturbance we would have seen had it not been for our almost daily efforts to help the mother hold herself together. The picture Carrie presented could not be explained simply as a result of overstimulation. Mrs. Ives provided many experiences a baby needs, but her inability to perceive Carrie's state meant that experiences were rarely presented at the right time or in the right way, resulting in deprivation of important growth promoting and organizing experiences. We were seeing a well-endowed infant's functioning deteriorate under the impact of poor care by parents who without doubt loved their child very much. The need for more help was clear.

Daycare and Other Remedies

About this time Mr. Ives had lost one of his part-time jobs, and Mrs. Ives was thinking about the need for her to find work. In this nonthreatening context we offered to have Carrie in daycare while her mother looked for a job. Although Carrie was brought only irregularly during the following weeks for a few hours at a time, she showed dramatic improvement in every way. Mrs. Ives had at first been reluctant about leaving Carrie with the daycare staff and initially said she would do so only if Mrs. S., her social worker, was going to be present, but she came to enjoy being there herself and quickly decided that Carrie liked the nursery and was consequently less difficult at home. Indeed, the nurturing of the mother by the daycare staff as well as by the social worker and pediatrician, along with Carrie's care in the program, seems to have interrupted the mounting tension between Mrs. Ives and Carrie at its height at the time of her 6-month evaluation.

After many unsuccessful attempts to find employment, Mrs. Ives worked briefly as a waitress but quickly decided she couldn't take the pressure, couldn't, as she said, manage a job along with the shopping, cleaning, and child care. She made reference to her psychiatric illness and was worried about a recurrence. Staff concern that this meant Carrie would no longer be brought to daycare was overshadowed by the parents' financial plight and the consequent decision to move out of state where work for Mr. Ives was thought to be available and they could live with Mrs. Ives's mother. Thus Carrie's daycare experience beginning at 7 months was interrupted after less than two months of sporadic attendance.

Four months later, after keeping in touch with Mrs. S. by mail, the family returned, pleased to rejoin the project. There had been many tensions in living in the big extended family, and Mr. Ives had not found work. Carrie, now 13 months old, was again entered into daycare so her mother could look for a job. When seen two months later for developmental evaluation at not quite 15 months, Carrie again showed striking improvement in all aspects of development, and her mother's behavior with her was far less intrusive and overwhelming. Also when visited at home Mrs. Ives was observed to play quite appropriately with Carrie, to help her use toys, and much more often to respond to the child's needs rather than her own.

During Carrie's two months in daycare Mrs. Ives again experienced her own enjoyment of the center. On one occasion she asked semihumorously if they could move in. Now she showed far less anxiety about Carrie and instead perceptible enjoyment of playing with her. This improvement in Mrs. Ives may have been due in part to Carrie's reaching a somewhat less vulnerable age in her mother's eyes. In addition, the support of the social worker, the pediatrician, and the daycare staff contributed to lessening Mrs. Ives's chronic anxiety. Reduced anxiety made it possible for her to make better use of child care counseling available to her from the beginning but seldom used. Fifteen months after Carrie's birth, while Mrs. Ives was clearly attached to those who worked with her, she was much less dependent on them for almost daily contact.

After the first year her use of the pediatrician was minimal but appropriate. Carrie had few illnesses, and Dr. P. was called only in the event of illness. At this time the social worker recorded the following: "In comparison with a year ago when Carrie was 3 months old, Mrs. Ives is functioning remarkably better in all areas. She is still a disturbed woman but her genuine delight and pleasure in Carrie are apparent and they do have good times together." To the extent that Mrs. Ives began to be influenced in her child care both by staff counseling and staff behavior with Carrie, it is likely that the basis of the change was mainly an identification with staff attitudes and behavior. One aspect of her personality was a persistent adolescent resistance to acknowledge that she used advice.

In staff discussion when Carrie was 15 months old there was a feeling of cautious optimism about the family. But suddenly Mrs. Ives lost her job and found another that required her to work at night. Illogically, she reasoned that she would then not need daycare for Carrie and predictably became increasingly fatigued and irritable as she tried to work nights and care for Carrie by day. Soon after a brief illness, she decided not to resume working. Though toddler school was now available to Carrie, Mrs. Ives brought her only a few times between 15 and 18 months. Each time Mrs. Ives lost a job or decided she couldn't manage one, she became depressed and anxious about a recurrence of her psychiatric illness. At such times she tended to lack the energy to come to the center consistently so that Carrie could be in toddler school or daycare. However, during this period (15 to 18 months) her improved functioning with Carrie continued, and Carrie again did well on her developmental exam at 18 months. She had become a toddler with a definite sense of herself. She expressed an age-appropriate range of feelings and was very clear about what she wanted and didn't want, what she would and would not do without a struggle. Although she presented her mother with some typical toddler negativism, the relationship, though a bit stormy at times, did not deteriorate. Mrs. Ives liked Carrie's assertiveness. She continued to enjoy Carrie and be pleased with all she was learning. It was Mr. Ives who could not accept what he considered Carrie's willfulness, and he and Mrs. Ives quarreled over his harshness with Carrie. He may, however, have provided some of the structure the child needed to offset her mother's relative disorganization. In spite of his frequent harshness. Carrie continued to be devoted to him and upset when he was away overnight.

Carrie Helps to Organize Her Mother

During the last year of the family's participation in the project, when Carrie was 18 to 30 months, their family life continued to be subject to stress due to insufficient income, accumulating bills, many moves from one inadequate apartment to another, and recurrent turbulence alternating with relative calm in the relationship of the couple. During this time Carrie was not in daycare and was only irregularly in toddler school. Mrs. Ives was no longer attempting to find employment. She was reconciled to her inability to function satisfactorily on a job, and it was clear that as long as she was at home, she needed Carrie with her. It was as if the child now was able to help organize her mother.

At the end of the project Mrs. Ives recalled how difficult the first months had been, when Carrie was completely dependent on her. She spoke of how much easier she found caring for Carrie when she became able to make her wants known and was old enough to be played with. For others Carrie had, of course, been unusually "readable" and able to be played with almost from the beginning. With minimal help from experiences in daycare and toddler school promoting her innate capacities and offsetting some of the turbulence at home, Carrie became a toddler whose way of expressing her wants and needs was graphic enough to be understood by her mother. This, in itself, was helpful in reducing some of Mrs. Ives's anxiety and enabling her to function a little better with Carrie. Also helpful was Mrs. Ives's unusual capacity to play with her child in a way that was enjoyable for both of them, suggesting that their future relationship might be more like one of siblings than of mother and daughter. Mrs. Ives recognized her greater comfort with Carrie's increasing independence and at the same time her own greatly reduced dependence on the project staff. During the last year she always welcomed the contacts with staff, especially the social worker, but did not seek more than her regularly scheduled appointments. (By contrast, once during the first year when the social worker had seen her every day for a week Mrs. Ives complained about not seeing her very often.) At termination Mrs. Ives could speak of missing the contacts but also recognize that she no longer needed them as she once had. With some pride she spoke of rearing Carrie differently than she had been reared: She didn't beat her, she played with her and enjoyed her, and said this had been her goal all along.

As for Carrie, judging from observations of her both at home and in the center, where she came during the last year regularly for physical and developmental examinations and irregularly to toddler school, she was developing far better than we had thought she might when she was 6 months old. The results of both her 24- and 30-month developmental assessments were about the same as at 18 months; that is, there was almost no scatter among the areas tested and she scored well within the average range. On the 30-month exam, she did a little less well than Dr. D. felt she could because of the characteristic that was an asset in interaction with her mother, being very definite in her likes, dislikes, and wishes. In a testing situation this meant that after minimal effort she rejected tasks that held low interest for her, and she was not easily persuaded to persist. However, she showed neglible anxiety, was self-confident, friendly, responsive to the examiner's praise, and enjoyed herself.

Follow-up

At follow-up five years later Mrs. Ives, who came from out of state to participate, described Carrie as intelligent and sensitive to other people's problems, highly competitive with other children and wanting always to be the best. The absence of her father, from whom the mother had been separated for several years, had been a problem for her. Carrie had been angry at her mother "for not producing him" and jealous of children who had fathers at home. When Carrie was "hurt" according to her mother, she withdrew into reading. Mrs. Ives spoke also of her pleasure in Carrie, of playing with her still. The impression she gave of their relationship was less that of mother and child than of companions.

Carrie was just 8 years old when tested at follow-up. She was a tall, slender, fair-skinned, freckle-nosed girl with an attractive, delicate face. She was immediately friendly in her manner toward the psychologist and during the test session was talkative, playful, and energetic. On the WISC-R her verbal IQ was 101, performance IQ 106, full scale IQ 103. Of special interest was the wide scatter on the subtests from two years below age to almost four years above age. She did especially well on the comprehension, picture arrangement, coding, and object assembly subtests, showing good concentration, pleasure, and imagination.

On the digit span, picture arrangement, and picture completion she made careless mistakes on simple items while passing more difficult ones, and it was not clear why this occurred except that she was responding very quickly and was invested in keeping a social contact with the examiner. The block design subtest was the only genuinely difficult task for her. When diagonals were introduced into the design she had trouble with orientation and scored two years below age. Similarly, while she scored well on the coding she tilted her paper in order to do the task. It may be that this and block performance reflected some mild difficulty in eye function (convergence, tracking, etc.) related to strabismus, for which she had had surgery. On the Beery Test of Visual Motor Integration she performed well and similarly on the Draw-A-Person Test. In addition Carrie's performance on the Peabody Individual Achievement Test in math, reading, reading comprehension, spelling, and general information were all above the scores expected for her age.

Carrie's mother commented on her high energy level and involvement in activity, and Carrie demonstrated her cheerleading and gymnastic skills for the psychologist. Nonetheless she was able to work through the hour and a half examination with one break in the middle of the session. She was both cooperative and playful, demonstrating considerable skill in exercising control of the situation in a socially acceptable way. While one would expect some degree of anxiety in a test situation in a child of 8 years, Carrie's anxiety was either minimal or well concealed behind her active, playful, energetic demeanor. The psychologist summed up her impressions of Carrie as follows:

> Carrie appears to be a most happy and playful child with a lively imagination. She demonstrates significant pleasure in carrying out the tasks of the examination and thoroughly enjoys her time. While she might frown when tackling a particularly difficult task, she does not seem upset by it, and, in fact, appears quite relaxed throughout the session. . . . She acknowledges the difficulty of some items and accepts failure without dismay. . . . She is playful in interaction with her mother, and her mother seems to clearly enjoy Carrie's playfulness, frequently smiling during the session. . . . Most attractive about Carrie are her energetic spunk and playfulness and her pleasure in both problem solving and interaction. She is so facile with her imagination and social playfulness, one might wonder on knowing her better whether such characteristics might be too prominent and interfere with her functioning. Within the context of a brief contact, however, such creativity and imaginativeness are quite delightful and charming.

Thus, Carrie's status at age 8 was reassuring. Her test scores did not indicate, as we had once feared, that living with her disturbed mother would lead to substantial difficulties in learning and in organization of behavior. The psychologist questioned whether Carrie's imagination, which appeared to be largely an asset and certainly made her appealing, was adequately anchored in a sense of reality.

This was a valid and relevant question, but we detected no major disturbance in her functioning at this time.

What was accomplished in the Ives case was important, in our view, though limited in scope. Project services did not change Mrs. Ives's basic disturbance, which will continue to affect her functioning both as an individual and as a mother. Five years after close of the project she was not among the parents who had materially improved their educational or socioeconomic status. Her life-style was very much the same except that she and Mr. Ives had separated and she was supporting herself and Carrie, something she had not been capable of doing during the project. Mrs. Ives had developed a number of new interests and was optimistic about the future. She had plans to marry a man she described as shy and sweet, a man Carrie liked. Carrie was still the only child, and Mrs. Ives's enjoyment of her was still evident. In contrast to Miss Galer of the previous case, Mrs. Ives used what the project offered in a very limited way. But it seems likely that without the almost daily support of staff during the first year and without the opportunity to use daycare at critical times, the state of both Mrs. Ives and Carrie would have become even more precarious than it was at six months after the child's birth.

CHAPTER 6

Empathy and Optimism:
Nurturing an Uncomfortable Baby

Mrs. Madison and Paul

Mrs. Madison, a 21-year-old black woman, had been married, but her husband left her when, after returning from Vietnam, he was unable to decide whether he or someone else had impregnated her. Mrs. Madison had quit school in the ninth grade. She was now supported mainly by welfare but had done factory work and practical nursing. She was a member of a very large and close extended family. She and her mother maintained a cordial relationship, and she once said, "I think my mother is wonderful even now." Mrs. Madison impressed project staff as being self-reliant, stoical, intelligent in practical, concrete matters, and well grounded in reality. She maintained high standards in relation to her grooming and housekeeping and in other ways as well showed an admirable degree of self-respect. However, during antepartum interviews she spoke of loneliness and seemed sad over the loss of her husband. We were concerned about her and about how her loneliness would affect the care of her child in spite of thinking that she had the potential to be a warm and wise mother. We were concerned about her, too, because the pregnancy was complicated by a sixty-five pound weight gain and toxemia, including intermittent elevated blood pressure and edema.

The Challenge of an Uncomfortable Infant

The condition of the infant at birth was to make mothering him both demanding and worrisome. Prior to delivery the baby had several episodes of distress as revealed in the fetal electrocardiogram. He was delivered after nineteen hours of labor with the cord around

96

neck and shoulders. (Apgar at one minute was 7; at five minutes, 10.) He weighed 5 lbs., 3 oz., a small-for-dates postmature, jaundiced infant. On the newborn examination, Paul, as he was named, was a tremulous infant, easily startled by outside stimuli and by his own spontaneous activity. His pediatrician, Dr. P., considered the central nervous system to be free from signs of damage. His autonomic nervous system was labile, and breathing, sucking, and swallowing were not well synchronized. He had a poor sucking response and a heart murmur. His mild jaundice had decreased at the time of discharge. His pediatrician considered him healthy, but a physiologically unstable, uncomfortable infant who would not be easy to care for.

Mrs. Madison and Paul were discharged on the fourth postpartum day. Their days at home were especially trying for his mother. She was exhausted and frightened after the first night, in which Paul had many jerking movements, was tremulous, was difficult to feed, was unable to sleep more than two hours at a time, and cried a great deal. Thus from the beginning he was an exceedingly difficult infant to care for because of the frequency and intensity of his discomfort, which he expressed in crying.

Initially Mrs. Madison channeled almost all of her concerns and complaints about Paul to the pediatrician via her social worker, Mrs. S. A little shy with Dr. P., Mrs. Madison was afraid that she would "bother the doctor too much." However, gradually reassured that Dr. P. wanted to be available to her, she made excellent use of pediatric help. Dr. P. had noted early that Paul could be comforted by firm holding and swaddling and sometimes was relieved of physiological distress by position change. As these observations were shared with Mrs. Madison, she was able to use them immediately and appropriately. She was advised not to let Paul cry very long because he became extremely tense and the crying accelerated. Nothing was heard from Mrs. Madison, as one might have heard from many mothers, regarding the danger of spoiling the baby by picking him up when he cried. Paul would take only about two ounces of formula at a time so he had to be fed often night and day. His digestive system, affected by his general body tension, also caused him distress. Thus it was suggested that he needed more frequent burping

than most babies, and again his mother was able to follow the pediatrician's suggestion.

The social worker, Mrs. S., became concerned about the fatigue
Mrs. Madison experienced in caring for this very difficult infant and
at one point insisted that she had to have some relief. The family
members visited often but were not offering to care for Paul. Once
her need for an occasional night's sleep was supported by Mrs. S.,
Mrs. Madison was able to ask for and get the family help she so
greatly needed. By the time of Paul's first-month physical exam he
was occasionally sleeping through the night. His weight gain and
growth were satisfactory. He was characterized as a physically tense
infant who still had some tremulousness and discoordinated jerky
movements but no evidence of neurological damage. By the 2½-
month exam his progress was quite reassuring. He was crying less
because he was obviously more comfortable. Considerable visual attention to people and inanimate objects was apparent. Also, in his
social awareness, responsiveness, and vocalization he was above age
level.

Progress but Miles to Go

Paul's progress during the especially difficult first three months was
due to several factors: Mrs. Madison's ability to accept suggestions
for relieving the infant's discomfort, the continuous availability of
support so that she did not feel alone with a potentially overwhelming problem, and her ability to hold and in other ways to care for
her baby in a relaxed way even though she was very worried about
him. If Paul had been the child of a mother who was normally very
tense, his mother's bodily tension would have heightened his own,
increasing the level of discomfort. Fortunately, Mrs. Madison's concern and feeling for Paul were manifested not in anxious, tense handling but in a comfort-giving, empathic kind of care. She read his
signals well and could adapt her handling to his need at the moment.
But it would still be a long time until Paul would no longer cause
concern and require special care.

It was hard for Mrs. Madison to talk about some of her more

anxiety-laden thoughts about her baby. But *we* found *her* signals easy to read. As some of the initial problems lessened, it was apparent that the heart murmur needed investigation, for her reasons as well as ours. The cardiac evaluation at 3 months was reassuring, and for the first time she was able not always to think of Paul as a sick baby. While her concerns during the first months were realistic, she became worried anew each time he had a respiratory infection or a digestive upset, and he had many beginning in the fourth month. On the assumption that helping Paul to be more active motorically would lessen his tremulousness and jerking, it was suggested at 7 months that he be placed for brief periods in a walker, which helped. He was 13 months old before his mother could count on his occasionally sleeping through the night, and he often did not during periods of illness.

Well into Paul's second year, whenever he was ill, some of his mother's early apprehension would recur. Out of her fatigue and despair, she would ask, "Will he ever be well, will he ever let me have a night's sleep?" When he was 16 months she said she felt as if she had not had a good night's sleep since he was born. Yet in our many observations of Mrs. Madison with Paul there was never any situation in which she exhibited resentment over the anguish and fatigue caring for him had involved. Despite her feeling that she had not slept through the night since his birth, there were periods that were relatively problem-free, and at such times what came through was her pride in Paul, her enjoyment of "how smart" he was and by 16 months "how cooperative in doing little chores." She reacted to some of his behavior with tolerant amusement, once for example commenting on how "considerate" he was to vomit over the side of his crib rather than on his bedding. Occasionally stress from some aspect of her life other than Paul's care caused her to be impatient and irritable with him, but these episodes never had the quality of a pervasive, retaliatory anger. Rather, they were expectable reactions in view of the temporary stress she was experiencing. At such times she needed a great deal of support from both Dr. P. and Mrs. S. and help in reducing the cause of distress. When suggestions were made during "good periods" about matters not specifically related to Paul's health but to child-care practices, she often seemed to lack interest. Yet later we would observe that she had incorporated what had been said into her way of responding to Paul. She made it her own and used it.

By the time Paul was 18 months he had come a long way toward overcoming his difficulties. On developmental evaluation at that time he scored within the average range, but more impressive was the overall good quality of his functioning. The developmental examiner, Dr. D., recorded:

> Paul . . . is willing to sit at the small table with his mother beside him and goes to work without apparent anxiety. His casual looks at me and acceptance of materials in the beginning change to increasing friendliness, grins, and sharing of pleasure as the hour progresses. He looks to his mother from time to time with a special knowing grin, and goes to her and leans against her when he gets up from the table. In comparison with his early tenseness and anxiety, Paul now appears relaxed, friendly, interested, and able both to enjoy motor skills and to sit quietly at tasks on the tabletop. He approaches tasks with interest and has an active and robust way of protesting when he has had enough.

Over the period of the project Mrs. Madison used to some degree all aspects of the available services, including daycare for Paul from his fifteenth to thirtieth month. Before the project ended he had become a sturdy, very masculine-looking little boy invested in physical activity and also interested in books. Except for his occasional respiratory infections, he was in good health. His performance on developmental evaluation at 30 months was, as before, within the average range.

Follow-up

At follow-up five years later, when Paul was 7½ years old, he again scored within the average range. On the WISC-R his verbal IQ was

101, performance IQ was 102, and full scale IQ 101. He was adequate on the Beery VMI test and did excellently on the Draw-A-Person. The reports of his scores on the Peabody Individual Achievement Test revealed that he was performing at an average level for his age in the areas tested: math, reading, reading comprehension, spelling, and general information. His mother reported that he had some difficulty in second grade, after doing well in first grade, but had "straightened out" in third grade. The psychologist who tested him at follow-up described him as amiable and as mildly anxious during the test. He was a little shy socially and did not ask for help but was able to use it when it was offered. He took pleasure in doing well.

At follow-up Mrs. Madison said, "I could never have survived those early difficult times without you." It is interesting that her memories of his infancy were mainly positive in spite of recalling how terrified she had been at his birth when she learned that he was in trouble. She added, "I know Paul was sickly but he had his nice times." She recalled, chuckling, how he first began to walk, how hard he tried to do so; that he first walked on his toes for some reason delighted her. Of Paul currently she reported that he had not been sick at all "since he was a baby" and had no eating or sleeping problems. She particularly liked his being an affectionate child, the fact that he was not "streetwise" and that he was interested, like herself, in sports.

Mrs. Madison was a young woman with a good amount of common sense and capacity for mothering. Had she given birth to a healthy infant, she would have had little need for project services. But it is well known that when a newborn is as difficult to care for as Paul was, the risk is great that discouragement, anger, and feelings of failure to cope with the infant may result in irreparable damage to the mother-child relationship, damage often continuing long after the early difficulties have been forgotten. Fortunately, because help was available when it was most needed, Paul and his mother came to have a trusting, affectionate relationship.

CHAPTER 7

Constricted Lives:
Mother and Child Play It Safe
Miss Keeler and Greg

In the case of Miss Keeler and her son, Greg, the focus is on the details of the relationship between Greg and his mother and on the child's development. Very early in Greg's life we were aware that Miss Keeler's style of mothering left much to be desired in its impoverishment of social and emotional communication, though there was no doubt that she was very interested in her child. He resembled, in many respects, the physically well cared for, experientially deprived institutionalized children reported by Provence and Lipton (1962). Miss Keeler's personality and character problems were reflected in the severe constriction of her emotional life, the narrow range of "safe" activities she allowed herself, and her excessive and at times paralyzing anxiety about physical illness. Unaccustomed to self-reflection, she appeared to accept herself pretty much as she was, with little or no motivation toward internal change, but she was keen on improving her living situation, especially her physical surroundings, and she expected to support herself and Greg as soon as she was able to do so. We do not know much about how these characteristics came about in her own development, since her recall for details of her childhood was meager and what little we learned about her early years came up primarily when her memories were stimulated by current events in her life.

Another point to be made in this case is that, while we were of some assistance to Miss Keeler and Greg, her utilization of services in comparison to need was much more selective and episodic than was true of any other family. We were well aware at all times that Miss Keeler needed the forms of help and support for child care we were prepared to provide, but our influence was more limited than we had hoped. In spite of this, she seems to have felt very much benefited by participation in the program.

Miss Keeler was a 20-year-old black woman who had grown up in the deep South, the seventh child and fifth girl in a family with twelve children. Both of her parents worked as farm laborers, her mother intermittently because of her many pregnancies. Her mother seems to have been a distant figure to Miss Keeler, who spoke more frequently of her grandmother and older sisters. She had finished high school but hadn't liked it and wasn't, she said, a good student. She came North to find work and be near one of her sisters. Her most sustained employment had been as a "live-in mother's helper" for a family with eight children, perhaps a replacement for her own large family.

We were not permitted to know the father of Miss Keeler's baby or to learn of her feelings about him beyond what appeared to be indifference, perhaps a defensive reaction to his lack of interest in her. She had been supported by public welfare for three months when she joined the study. At the time of Greg's birth she was sharing an apartment with a friend, Miss Vance, her 15-month-old son, and a newborn girl. Miss Keeler reported that they shared responsibilities for the apartment and helped each other in times of need.

A Promising Newborn—Early Hints of Later Trouble

Greg was born one week prior to term weighing 5 lbs., 8 oz. When examined by the pediatrician at the age of 6 hours he was characterized as small in size but well developed, mature, well organized motorically, and easily comforted. There were no physical signs of prematurity. Rooting and sucking responses were vigorous and all other newborn reflexes were present and normal. His cry was lusty, sustained, and normal in pitch and he could be comforted by holding and cuddling and being given something to suck. The pediatrician did not talk with Miss Keeler until the third postpartum day because she had been pre-eclamptic and was kept in quiet seclusion and sedated immediately postpartum. At this visit she had just fed the baby, who was asleep in her room, and she asked a number of questions about him. But she focused most, in her talk with the pediatrician that day, on her concerns about herself, including her confusion and anxiety about why she was alone in the room, with tasteless food and other restrictions. Observations of Greg by the pediatrician, Dr. P., and a second staff member over the period of the five days of hospitalization continued to give the impression of a well formed, healthy, vigorous newborn with very well organized behavior. House calls to check the baby and to talk with Miss Keeler were made when he was 1 week and 2 weeks of age and were unremarkable: Miss Keeler asked appropriate questions about his physical care and listened to the pediatrician's responses. She volunteered in one of these visits that she didn't believe in rocking babies "because it spoils them," and that she didn't hold the baby very much. Dr. P. commented at the end of the report of the second visit that she had not seen Miss Keeler cuddle the baby; she preferred to hold him out on her lap in an upright position.

On their first clinic visit when Greg was 5 weeks old, he was characterized as a well-developed baby who had gained almost three pounds over his birth weight. Both weight and height were at the third percentile on the growth charts. He was alert, following objects visually, but was relatively inactive motorically. It was observed that while Miss Keeler seemed to have good physical contact with the baby and to handle the changing and dressing deftly and gently, it was not clear how much other contact was involved. The pediatrician wrote, "She does not appear to be a good observer or reporter about the baby's behavior, and we must rely largely on our own observations for determining the extent and type of contact between mother and infant." Miss Keeler's discomfort and squeamishness when Dr. P. treated granulation tissue at the umbilicus were also noted. This was the first clue to what we were to observe many times later, that the physical examinations were stressful for Miss Keeler, perhaps because of some apprehension of what might be found, and concern about illness, both Greg's and her own, was a theme around which most of her utilization of our services occurred.

At the age of 9 weeks and 2 days Greg's developmental age was 12 weeks and his developmental quotient 129, indicating very good development and a well balanced profile. He was described as an active baby with strong, vigorous movements who looked well organized and alert. Head control was good and he assisted in the pull to sit situation. Prone behavior was less advanced than supine but still quite normal. He had spontaneous and responsive social smiles. He was alert, looked around when carried, and showed a great deal of interest in people. He also demonstrated good drive and energy toward the test materials for a baby of his age. He did not vocalize very much. When he did, it was primarily responsively, but the sounds were normally differentiated (musical cooing, etc.). The range of his affective expression was considered normal. His mother was observed to clean and change him gently and expertly but with very little social communication expressed either through the type of physical handling or through smiling or talking with him. The only indicators at this time of less than excellent development were that Greg did not react adaptively to the feeding situation and did not cuddle when handled by the examiner. In addition, he smiled more often at the examiner than at the mother, a very unusual occurrence for a baby of this age.

The Gradual Decline

The first clear signs that Greg's development was beginning to suffer were noted on his three-month developmental and pediatric examinations. At 13 weeks and 2 days the developmental age was 15 weeks, 2 days, and the developmental quotient 114. He was still described as a healthy looking, handsome boy, very active and vigorous, with good head control. While he was visually active and alert he had not progressed as expected in reaching out with hands and arms toward people and objects and he was less interested in toys than before. At this time speech development was good: There was much vocalization, primarily in response to stimulation, but at times spontaneously as he vocalized to the toys, to his mirror image, and to other persons. He was noted to be *very* interested in watching the mother and others in the room though he showed no displeasure at the loss of social contact. The range of affective expression was described as moderate. He seemed aware of the developmental examiner, Dr. D., as a stranger, but he did not seem anxious. One of his noteworthy characteristics at this time was his tendency to become less active motorically when he felt uneasy. While he reacted with vigorous avoidance movements to the otoscopic exam, he otherwise was unusually passive during the physical examination. No thumb sucking was seen, and no hand play. His motor activity, while vigorous, was more diffuse and unfocused than one would have expected from a child whose neuromotor organization had been so excellent earlier. These observations gave rise to the speculation that Greg was not receiving enough stimulation to facilitate his investment in and awareness of his body. This hypothesis was consistent with the observations of the mother's style of interaction with him: There was a lack of vigor and variety in both her physical and social contacts with Greg, and an in-and-out quality about her attention to him. What we observed was similar to other observations about interferences in the early development of the body ego, awareness of body boundaries, and organization of the body scheme seen in experientially deprived children (Provence and Lipton 1962). We were reminded of Schilder's (1935) hypothesis, "But there is no question that our own activity is insufficient to build up the image of the body. The touches of others, the interest others take in different parts of our body, will be of enormous importance in the development of the postural model of the body" (p. 126).

Greg was reported to be eating well, sleeping through the night and taking several naps during the day, probably sleeping more hours than most babies of his age would do. He spent much time in an infant seat. His weight was at the 60th percentile and length at the 50th percentile.

By the time Greg was four months old, the impression of observers was that his mother showed genuine interest in and concern for him but was not adept at understanding his needs at a given moment. She focused very much on keeping him fed, clean, and dry according to her own schedule, which might or might not coincide with his needs. At about this time it became apparent that Miss Keeler was worried about her health. She had lost weight, complained of headaches and "nerves," was having trouble sleeping, and had a very poor appetite. Initial attempts to persuade her to seek medical care were unsuccessful. When Greg was 5 months old, her extreme fearfulness about illness and hospitals was vividly expressed in a discussion with the pediatrician. She was afraid she had cancer or some other life-threatening illness. As she became more preoccupied and self-involved, she was even less available to Greg than before. While her worry was, of course, entirely understandable, it had an adverse impact on Greg, whose mirroring of his mother's depressive affect at the 8-month contact was impressive. Miss Keeler commented that neither she nor Greg had an appetite but that she always ate better when her friend Miss Vance cooked than when she cooked for herself. She could speak of Greg's food preferences, but she was unobservant about sounds he could make. It was clear that there was little interchange involving mutual imitation. It was noted that Miss Vance was more socially involved with Greg than his mother was, that she provided much of his care, and that her presence was fortunate for him. During this period Greg's development both as measured by the tests at 6 and 9 months and as manifested in qualitative aspects of behavior continued to decline, and we became quite concerned about him.

At the age of 26½ weeks (6 months) Greg's developmental age was 25 weeks and his developmental quotient was 93—a decline in the test score. In contrast to his good trunk control for his age at an earlier examination, he now slumped when placed in sitting position and was also rocking. While he was able to pull to stand, he did no bouncing and had little motor drive, a marked contrast to his vigorous movement earlier. His performance in the adaptive area was adequate for his age: He demonstrated good interest in the toys, even showing a little displeasure at the loss of a particular toy though he easily accepted a substitute. His vocalizations were very sparse and language development had slumped, although not severely. He needed a great deal of activation to get him going about almost everything. The lack of pleasurable interchange between child and mother on this day was striking. In dressing him his mother was again characterized as gentle and skillful but detached. At one point she scolded him and spanked his leg because he had scratched the crib mattress with his fingernails when the pediatrician was out of the room. Greg was described as responsive when a friendly person approached him but lacking initiative in making social contact. There was much mouthing of toys but no thumb sucking. He made extensive use of the pacifier, which his mother obviously preferred him to mouth rather than his hands or the toys. His weight was at the 30th percentile.

Ups and Downs

In the period between Greg's fourth and eighth month the social worker had continued to work with Miss Keeler toward the goal of having a thorough physical examination. Near the end of this period we had become increasingly alarmed about Miss Keeler's almost marasmic condition. After considerable preparation concerning what she would need to tell the physician and with the social worker, at her request, accompanying her, Miss Keeler finally sought medical care. Her relief at learning that she had no serious disease was dramatic and her mood improved substantially. When Greg was seen at age 9 months, a few weeks later, it was clear that his mood was also more lively and he was more active physically. But there continued to be signs that his development was suffering in some respects from the experiences related to his mother's style of child care, with its narrow range of affective communication, meager stimulation for speech development, minimal playful interaction of any sort, and her use of scolding and spanking to restrict his motor activity and his mouthing.

The picture was mixed: Greg showed improvement in affective development in that his affective expressions were better differentiated and more easily recognizable, but there continued to be less variety and robustness than one would consider healthy. For example, responses indicating pleasure were recognizable but relatively subdued; he obviously enjoyed some of the toys but had less interest and zestful involvement than one expects at this age; he reacted with distinct displeasure once a toy was removed, but in a way that suggested disappointment rather than the usual, normal sounds of outrage. Motor development was good in that he could sit alone, creep, pull to stand, and cruise at the cribside. However, he made less use than one would expect of his ability to move about, either to get something he wanted or to avoid an unpleasant stimulus—a reflection, we assumed, of some inhibition in use of skills available to him, a deficit in ego functioning. Hand and finger skills were well developed. His performance in the adaptive area revealed a wide scatter from a low of two months below age to one month above. Here, too, one saw forward development reflecting his good native endowment; one also saw worrisome delays or distortions. Deficits seen were his failing to uncover the hidden toy, his lack of investigatory behavior, and the absence of signs of ability to combine two or more objects. The failure to search for the hidden toy indicated a delay in the development of object permanence in the Piagetian sense and was based, we assume, as in other infants we have studied, on deficits in the mother-child relationship. The lack of investigatory behavior suggested a less than normal investment of interest in the toys and other inanimate objects with a concomitant delay in that dimension of cognitive development. The failure to combine objects—that is, to bring them into relationship with one another—suggested a delay in the organization of behavior believed to be of importance in the development of integrative mental functions (Provence 1966). Thus, these findings suggested more clearly than before that Greg's future intellectual development might suffer in some respects. We were concerned, too, about the fact that his speech development was delayed. He had no name for his mother, though he clearly preferred her to others and was able to make the necessary sounds. Again, it was important that the kind of reinforcement that would facilitate the development of speech in a maturationally intact child was very sparse in Greg's experience, and we were not able to influence his mother to talk to him more. Socially, Greg continued to be responsive if a friendly person initiated social contact and play with him; that is, he could be "energized" to interact with clear enjoyment, but he took little initiative in creating social contact. It was apparent, also, that Greg was comforted by physical contact with his mother when he sat on her lap or she held him at her shoulder, but not much seemed to go on between them at a distance. Thus we were now even more concerned about long-term effects of the maternal style and the deficits in experience on Greg's emotional and cognitive development.

Daycare—Limited Benefits

We invited Miss Keeler to use our daycare program for a few hours a week because we felt that we could provide important supplements to Greg's daily experience, and when he was 11 months old, she accepted. On the day of admission he was described as indiscriminately friendly, mild in his responses to people, sometimes solemnly watchful and quiet. He had a little artificial laugh that seemed to be an indication of tension. About a week after admission there was one episode of his crying in a heartbroken way without any known provocation from the outside, and it took a long time for his special caregiver to comfort him.

As Greg appeared in the daycare setting between 11 and 30 months his fortunes fluctuated considerably. His mother grew comfortable and friendly with the daycare staff and seemed to value what the program could offer Greg. At the same time his attendance was episodic and appeared dependent upon how she felt in the morning and what her own plans were. When Greg was 14 months old she accepted a live-in job for a week and he stayed with relatives. During this time in daycare he became much less mobile, was listless and apathetic, ate without interest, and was mainly subdued or sad. We learned a few weeks later that she had taken him off both his bottle and pacifier at about the same time, though she would occasionally give him the bottle at bedtime. At the home visits the social worker noted that Greg stayed very close to his mother. She held him on her lap much of the visit, partly, it appeared, because both she and Greg enjoyed it and partly to control his moving about. She expressed fear that he would get lead poisoning if she allowed more freedom. Mother and child on that occasion seemed to enjoy each other in their quiet, understated way. She acknowledged that Greg wanted her and enjoyed her attention; however, even after everyone else recognized that he was calling her mama, she wasn't sure he meant her—a comment that perhaps reflects her uncertainty that she could be that important to him.

When Greg was 15 months old, Miss Keeler's grandmother, who was an important person to her, died, and this stress plus the discovery of a breast cyst (found to be benign) caused Miss Keeler's headaches, sleep problem and weight loss to recur; she was more detached from Greg and at the same time more harsh when his behavior displeased her. She began to go out more in the evenings, apparently to help herself feel better. There was no doubt that this was a difficult time for Greg, too, and he developed another symptom seen in disturbed children, namely eating dirt and other foreign substances. (Cooper 1957, Millikan et al. 1968, Leonard 1971.)

At the time of his 18-month developmental examination Greg's developmental age was 18 months and his developmental quotient was 100, an average score. The most noteworthy aspects of this session were qualitative: He was very involved in maintaining social contact and had a far less than healthy amount of autonomy and free energy for play and use of the materials. He seemed to enjoy the give and take with the examiner, seemed unafraid, and appeared moderately happy and contented. When stimulated he smiled, jargoned, and appeared animated but was again characterized as having somewhat muted affect. He had a selective interest in toys, that is, not all to the same degree, but there was no special interest or attachment to any of them, and the investment in them was not intense though his attention span was good. He would make a few attempts at achieving a goal in relation to materials but easily gave up. He did not become angry and expressed only a mild satisfaction at success. He seemed to have little interest in the process of problem solving and was very dependent upon the adult to involve him in such activities. His mother was quite stern with him, obviously wanting him to behave properly. He was very aware of her throughout and checked on her presence frequently. His vocabulary of four to six words placed his language within the average range for his age, reflecting considerable improvement since the last evaluation.

When Greg was 20 months of age he and his mother moved into the apartment the mother had been seeking with the help of her social worker for many months. It was a new, clean, recently finished place, and when she and Greg were seen when he was 21 months for his pediatric exam, she looked very well and was described as cheerful, animated, almost euphoric, and very happy about their new home, which she had worked hard to furnish. It was extremely orderly with virtually nothing in sight that would be of interest to a young child, and there was no doubt that the activity and curiosity expected in a child of Greg's age had to be subordinated to his mother's need for neatness and lack of clutter. Again, it was impressive how much she valued a clean, quiet child; even his low-keyed and inhibited expression of normal toddler interests and activities caused her to characterize him as bad and spoiled. He was attending daycare about half time though irregularly, and those who saw him both at home and in the center commented on his greater contentment and comfort at home. He gradually became more comfortable and willing to stay when brought in the morning but was always ready to leave by the time he was called for. His mother felt that he missed the children when he was home, but she found it difficult to understand that he missed her while at school. A daily half-day stay was far preferable for Greg and we tried hard to work this out, but it was not possible to do so because Miss Keeler never accepted that it would be better for Greg if she picked him up earlier. Her view was that one treated crying and longing for someone by being tough and soon the child would get over it. It was at naptime that he seemed to feel the separation from his mother most deeply and he needed much comfort. It appeared that he was viewed somewhat neutrally by his peers, as neither an aggressor nor a particularly interesting companion. He was, however, a sociable child with the others and was among the first to call others by name. He appeared to like them and joined in some play with them. Greg was the child most likely at this time to make first contact with a visitor, often approaching with outstretched arms. He knew all the caregiving staff very well but rarely called them by name. His attachment to staff members was tenuous at best and he rarely sought out a particular person. He could be angry when his wishes were thwarted, but even his anger was somewhat despairing. He could fight back to some degree if aggressed against, but he was easily overwhelmed by the normal aggressive behavior of other children.

There were no remarkable changes in Greg or his mother during the remainder of the project. Miss Keeler continued to like her new home and worked part-time. During the last few months of his time with us Greg was described by the daycare staff as physically competent; he had also developed adequate language. Yet there was a disturbing quality in his social relationships and in his play. He seemed to have little creative energy, little ability to use toys or explore materials in any but the most superficial way. This was characteristic of his interaction with people also: a surface friendliness that was rather pleasant until one realized that it was without depth and with little specificity except in relation to his mother. One thing Greg did enjoy was motor activity, and he spent a lot of outdoor time riding scooters. He was well coordinated and the first child to master a tricycle. He liked looking at books and would name familiar objects when he saw them. During several months when he was between 22 and 28 months of age there were many notes by the daycare staff about his aggressive behavior toward others. He seemed unhappy much of the time and very much at odds with himself and those around him. Even in his better times he had little to contribute to even the most simple dramatic play. He liked to use the dress-up clothes and had a favorite hat and wallet and bag which he chose from the shelf. He would then stand in the middle of the floor, the embodiment of the phrase "all dressed up with no place to go." He could participate when a teacher structured a pretend situation such as taking a walk or going on a bus or sitting down to eat in the housekeeping corner, but he went along rather mechanically. Using the toy telephone was one of the few instances in which he could be involved in a little bit of fantasy play.

At 2½ he was growing well, being somewhat tall and slender for his age with height at the 75th percentile and weight at the 25th percentile. His mother proudly reported at his 2½-year evaluation that he was now toilet trained both day and night. On testing, Greg's developmental age was 29.2 months and his developmental quotient 99, with scores ranging from 24 to 36 months. Language was at 30 months. Problem solving at 25 months was probably a minimal score owing to his lack of interest in pursuing anything at all difficult. His affect ranged from brief moderate pleasure to sadness, disappointment, and some anger, but nothing was expressed with intensity or zest. The lack of robustness in his affective responses suggested far from optimal emotional development. Dr. D.'s report of the evaluation concluded as follows: "His minimal ability to use toys or other materials with any great interest—seen both in the daycare and testing situations—is an indicator, I believe, of a constriction of his emotional life. While he seems intelligent enough, it is difficult to know how he will get along later in school."

At the end of the contact with Greg and his mother we found his mother reasonably well satisfied with her life and with her son. She was working part-time, seemed to be feeling fairly well physically most of the time and expressed much more satisfaction with Greg now than when he was younger. It may be that his ability to walk and talk and his compliance with her training made the task of child rearing seem much less overwhelming to her.

Efforts to Help Miss Keeler, a Resumé

One might ask, in respect to Greg and his mother, how intensive was the effort to assist them and what were the specific services offered. As indicated earlier, in spite of continuing efforts we were less effective than we had hoped to be. Both social worker and pediatrician had many contacts with Miss Keeler, sometimes at her request, sometimes in the course of the scheduled visits agreed upon between parents and staff. Our initial impression of Miss Keeler as an anxious, depressed person with many psychosomatic symptoms (anorexia, headaches, backaches, weight loss, palpitations, insomnia, listlessness) was correct. As reported, confirmation was provided when Greg was 8 months old by the very thorough physical examination she allowed the social worker to arrange, but only after weeks of work on her anxiety about it. Both knowledge that her symptoms were due to depression, not disease, and the antidepression medication briefly prescribed were of help to her in that she began to feel better and look better, as described earlier. The trend toward better health and appearance continued to the end of the study. She had a few setbacks when she again needed help to prepare for an appointment at the medical center and needed Mrs. S. to accompany her. Miss Keeler looked to Mrs. S. to help her not only around her own illnesses but with her anxiety when a relative or friend was ill or died. Toward the end of the study she asked for and received psychological counseling and assistance in arranging an abortion for an unwanted pregnancy.

At no time was Miss Keeler able to respond to efforts to help her explore her tendency to substitute physical symptoms for psychic pain or to help her cope more effectively with her severe anxiety about anything to do with illness. Her anxiety was not only upsetting but disabling, compounding her worry about herself and her child. Once, when she had reason to be concerned that Greg might have lead poisoning, she repeatedly failed to keep appointments for his blood tests. She relied in most ways on Dr. P. for Greg's health care and followed advice when he was ill. Yet, there were times when paradoxically she ignored advice—for example, failed to complete a course of antibiotics and remained uninfluenced by the pediatrician's explanation of why it was important to give all the medication prescribed.

Several times reference has been made to Miss Keeler's strong wish to get better housing. Although success in this way was very important to her, a tremendous amount of support from Mrs. S. over a period of months was required in order for Miss Keeler to make and persist in following through on an application to a new housing project. In matters that were less important to her, similar staff efforts were not successful. After starting Greg in daycare at 11 months, she came to like and trust the teachers and to think the program was good for him. But she brought him irregularly and could not be persuaded to provide a more consistent experience. Similarly, when Greg's development began to lag, many attempts were made to help Miss Keeler stimulate him in specific ways. But these efforts were largely ineffectual mainly because the impoverishment of her own personality did not allow her to see her child as a person with unique capacities and needs. In contrast with other mothers in the study she was rarely open to thinking about individual development, and her main emphasis at all points was on having a physically healthy, neat, clean, and polite child who "cooperated" with her. Her unavailability to respond to these many efforts was clearly due to her personal rigidity, which made her largely unable to consider new ideas or optional methods of child care. Her rigidity was not caused by cultural tradition, socioeconomic status, or lack of intelligence. We assume that the lack of richness of Miss Keeler's affective life, originating in her own apparently lonely childhood, bore a relationship to the limitations in her capacities for empathy and emotional communication with her child.

Throughout the contact with Miss Keeler we were convinced that her conscious concern for her child was genuine, that he was important to her, and that she wanted to see that he received the things that in her view constituted the good life. It was abundantly clear that she experienced their participation in the study as contributing in significant ways to that goal. Yet there was a substantial gap between what the program offered and what Miss Keeler could utilize.

Follow-up

When Greg and his mother were seen for follow-up when he was 8½ years old they were living in the same housing development in a larger apartment, which was tastefully furnished and, as the visitor said, ". . . had a sort of elegance without much personal touch." Miss Keeler had been working as a nurse's aide for about a year, following a year and a half as a teacher's assistant in a daycare center for 3 to 5 year olds. She had received some training for each of these positions and reported that she liked both of them, preferring the current one because of better pay. She said that she had been in very good health with no recurrence of the symptoms she had when we knew her. Greg had been well, too, except for occasional colds and an accident in which his leg was broken at age 7 in a baseball game. She stopped work to stay home with him at that time. She described him as well developed in every way, as a child who got along well with her and with his friends, worked out his own disagreements, and had given no trouble. He had been in public school during kindergarten and first and second grade, but his mother transferred him to a parochial school because she felt he wasn't learning enough. She was very pleased with her choice and with his progress, which was especially good in spelling and arithmetic. When asked about her early memories of Greg Miss Keeler talked mainly about his medical history, remembering that he had many colds. When pressed to remember what he was like as a baby she described him as "not a bad baby," one who did not cry unless he was wet, hungry, or sleepy. The current characterizations were put in much the same terms: that he is good, happy, no trouble, gets along well, likes school. She reported that she was planning to be married to a man whom she had known for several years. The interviewer had the impression that she liked and enjoyed Greg and cared for him in a responsible way. The interviewer commented that there was more pleasure and animation in her voice as she spoke about him than there was when he was much younger. She herself looked strikingly better than when we knew her. She had gained a little weight and had an air of cheerfulness and well-being, more poise and self-esteem than she had had in the earlier days. She was very cordial and hospitable to the interviewer, and it was the impression that she was functioning better both as a person and as a mother than she had earlier.

The follow-up examination of Greg in the Child Development Unit included the WISC-R, the Beery Test of Visual Motor Integration, and the Draw-A-Person Test. He was 8 years and 6 months at the time of the evaluation, done by a person who had not seen him before. He was described as follows:

A handsome child of medium height and slim, Greg was particularly well dressed and clean. He sat very still, not at all restless, for the entire session. There was a gentle, precise quality about him in that his words were soft and well articulated and a smooth, precise and gentle quality as he moved puzzle pieces or blocks on the table. In the waiting room he was observed to carefully put the toys away before walking quietly and calmly to the testing room. He smiled gently at times. He scowled or sighed when having difficulty in solving a problem. There was little enthusiasm about anything but rather a slightly muted quality to his affect. More than the other children tested he was able to comfortably acknowledge that he did not know answers without appearing to become anxious. He performed best on rote tasks such as arithmetic, digit span, and certain factual questions, and he did less well on tasks necessitating more active analysis and integration.

Greg was quiet yet responsive and warm without being outgoing or spontaneous. He was well behaved at all times, and one sensed that he was there to do what was asked of him. While he did not actively seek the support of the examiner he responded to reassurance from her. He looked at his mother a few times during the session, sometimes glancing and checking her out and at other times extending the contact and sharing a smile with her.

On the Beery VMI his age equivalent was 5 years and 7 months. He worked quietly and seriously on the test, forming the shapes slowly. He had particular difficulty in the coordination of intersections. On the WISC-R he had a full scale IQ of 85 with a verbal IQ of 96 and a performance IQ of 75. Of more interest than the overall score, however, was the performance on the subtests. On the information subtest, for example, his successes fit a pattern in which he had difficulty with questions whose answers are based on experience and did better with information usually gathered by rote memory. The subtests on which he scored at an age adequate level or better were arithmetic, where he had an age equivalent of 10½ years, and digit span, where he had an age equivalent of 12½ years. He showed skill and adeptness at arithmetic calculation and was able to translate word problems into the numerical form and solve them. Needing little time to think, indicating that he knew his "tables" well, he succeeded solidly with the first eleven items and one more difficult problem. He concentrated well on the digit span task and his repetitions of the sequences were smooth and prompt. The psychologist commented, "That he does so well on the test of short-term memory is in accord with the strengths in his other performance, which center around knowledge which is often memorized." Greg's performance on the picture arrangement and picture completion subtests and the block design were below the 6 year level, with coding and object assembly close to his age and with similarities, vocabulary and comprehension subtests in the 7 to 7½ year range. On the vocabulary subtest he defined an appropriate number of words for his age yet obtained only partial credit on a number of them because his definitions were simple and not adequately elaborated. Similarly, with the comprehension questions it was clear that he had an understanding of the situations inquired about, but his answers were insufficient for full credit. He had trouble with the picture arrangement and block design, reflecting some difficulty in analyzing causal and temporal sequences; he tended to describe or approach each picture or design as a separate entity. His drawing of a person was primitive for his age, with simple features, poorly integrated, and lacking in detail. In contrast to this immature and poorly developed human figure drawing was his signature at the top of the paper, where quite beautifully and evenly he wrote his full name in script.

Compliance—Advantages and Disadvantages

It was not difficult to recognize in Greg at age 8½ many of the characteristics that were seen at 2½ years and earlier. Miss Keeler seemed quite satisfied with her life and felt very good about herself and her son. She gave great credit to the project, emphasizing particularly her gratitude for the medical care and the daycare. One of the remarkable findings at the time of the follow-up was the extent to which she had succeeded in producing, at least as far as Greg's external behavior is concerned, precisely the kind of child of which she most approved. And perhaps since she seemed happy at this point with him and he with her, it could be asked whether anything more should be wished. However, we are compelled to emphasize that while Greg was at this time a compliant, conforming child who was performing adequately in school and doing quite well in some respects, it seems likely that he will not realize anything like the intellectual and emotional capacity with which he appeared to have been endowed. He has adapted well and conformed thus far to his mother's standards and expectations. He and his mother appeared quite content with one another, mutually approving and loving. But both in his intellectual development and in his affective life there appear to be deficits and constrictions, very much like those apparent when he was 2½. Cognitively he is best with the stable, sure things: numbers, memorized information, rules. Tasks requiring analysis and synthesis are more difficult. Academic performance may become more problematic as he grows older and there is greater need for flexibility, versatility, and creativity. We have a less detailed view of Greg's emotional development at 8½ years and therefore should be careful about comparisons with earlier times. What we can safely say is that according to his mother he manages peer relationships adequately. His politeness and good behavior no doubt make him attractive to his teachers and other adults. This conformity to maternal standards appears ego-syntonic. If he has struggled much against them, it is not apparent, though, of course, we have no direct data on the 2½ to 8½ year period. The limitations on his intellectual development and the apparent constriction of his emotional development are, in our view, experiential in origin and stem primarily from characteristics of the maternal personality and style of child care and from the mother-child relationship, which we could influence in only a very limited way.

CHAPTER 8

Captives of the Past:
Struggling toward Freedom
Mrs. O'Neal and Joan

In sharp contrast to the background of other study mothers was that of Mrs. O'Neal. An articulate, intelligent, emotionally disturbed young woman, she was the oldest of four girls in a white, middle-class family. Her father was a YMCA executive and a member of the school board. Her mother was a librarian. Both parents were active in causes related to education and especially educational opportunities for those of minority races. The professional identity and activities of her parents were significant because of their influence on some of the ways in which Mrs. O'Neal's disturbance was manifested and affected the care of her child, Joan.

Mrs. O'Neal had lived at home until dropping out of college in the first year. She had been living in an apartment of her own for two years when we first met her at age 21. She was married but separated from her husband, and during interviews for admission to the project spoke of her intention to divorce him. She had held a number of jobs since leaving home but when interviewed for the study was supported by public welfare, living under conditions of poverty and about to become the mother of an infant we judged would be at risk without intervention. Thus she was eligible for the study.

Why this intelligent young woman from a seemingly stable middle-class family was living in the inner city at a subsistence level was understandable not because of socioeconomic deprivation but because of her psychological disturbance. Our knowledge of Mrs. O'Neal's history and her feelings about her life and our speculation about her functioning in relation to that history developed only gradually over the months as she struggled to work out her problems. Even though they were serious, they were not to impinge as much as expected on her care of Joan owing in large part to the use she made of project services. The case report illustrates the ways in which Mrs. O'Neal's psychological disturbance was manifested in the early years of her child's life and the ways she utilized the services of the project, coordinated with the data on the development of her well-endowed girl child. The report begins with a summary of experiences in her life before joining the project which we assume to be of special relevance. They were revealed to us over many months, mainly from her own memories, augmented by answers to questions she raised with her mother.

A Turbulent Past

The firstborn of her parents, as an infant Mrs. O'Neal had remained in the hospital for a month after birth because her mother was ill and couldn't care for her, an occurrence that possibly interfered with the important processes of attachment and mutual adaptation between mother and infant. (Erikson 1959, Barnett et al. 1970, Kennell et al. 1970, Seashore et al. 1973, Brazelton 1974, Leiderman and Seashore 1975, Klaus and Kennell 1976). Her parents, especially her father, had wanted a boy and had chosen a name for a boy but not for a girl. She remained nameless for several months. At age 3, when her first sibling was about to be born, she was sent to relatives several hundred miles away. She had cried in terror all the way there. She regarded this extrusion from her home as a significant turning point, after which she became, she said, "a terrible child," angry, destructive, and uncontrollable. She also recalled overeating at an early age to the point of obesity and continuing to overeat through grade and high school. She spoke little of her relationship to her mother and concentrated mainly on her stormy relationship to her father. To him she attributed most of her problems, and this relationship was the one she was motivated to work on in her social work appointments. At age 5 Mrs. O'Neal experienced what she considered the psychological loss of her father to her younger sister, then age 2. She feared her father as an unpredictable, explosive, and potentially violent man, but she seems to have sought his love both for its own sake and for safety from his anger. Like many children, in the face of danger she became not meek and obedient but overly aggressive. Also at age 5 her aggressive behavior caused trouble with both her teacher and other children. There began her passionate hatred of several teachers and her low opinion of many over the years. All through grade and high school she was a rebellious misfit, never got a grade above C, had no friends, hated school. There followed an abortive attempt at college in which she failed all courses, the move away from home, and the attempt to support herself. Whether she did, in fact, "lose" her father after an early period of closeness we could not be sure. Regardless of the objective reality, the psychological truth for Mrs. O'Neal as a young adult was that her father had deserted her in childhood. She felt alienated from him, longed for his concern, but was so angry at him that she could not try to win his approval and could gain his attention, she felt, only by picking fights.

Turbulence in Marriage

Shortly after leaving home Mrs. O'Neal met the man she was later to marry. He was of mixed racial background, having a Puerto Rican mother and a black father who had disappeared before his birth. His mother, whom he called a prostitute and an alcoholic, had had a series of alliances with men whose violent, brutal behavior with her he had witnessed, and he himself had been beaten by some of them. He had dropped out of school in the ninth grade and was very nearly illiterate though with some aspirations for more education. His life story both horrified and fascinated Mrs. O'Neal. She saw in him someone who, like herself, had been mistreated, and she was drawn to him by his willingness to use her as a kind of mentor. But the marriage was in trouble almost from the beginning: it was characterized by quarreling and frequent physical assaults on Mrs. O'Neal, separations and reunions both before and after the divorce a year later. Information that led us to be concerned both for her and the coming infant she gave spontaneously during an interview before admission to the study: Seven or eight months earlier Mr. O'Neal had sought revenge for some presumed transgression of hers through an act of horrible cruelty to an animal she valued. In response to her anger over what he had done, he swung at her with a cleaver. She told of this experience without affect and with no apparent perception of how bizarre and dangerous Mr. O'Neal's behavior had been. She explained her subsequent pregnancy as resulting, in spite of being on the pill, from having been forced to submit to Mr. O'Neal sexually or be beaten. A month thereafter, when Mr. O'Neal in an outburst of anger threatened her with a knife and she fled to a friend's home, she still would have taken no action against him, but her friend, frightened for her, insisted on calling the police. He was arrested and later placed in a mental hospital where his diagnosis was schizophrenic reaction, paranoid type. He remained in the hospital during the third to sixth months of Mrs. O'Neal's pregnancy. After his release he did not again live with Mrs. O'Neal but was frequently with her. She expressed approval of his getting help with his problems and said that he was better. He was in attendance at the hospital when Joan, a healthy, full-term infant, was born. She was described by the pediatrician as an attractive, healthy, small baby girl, well proportioned and well formed. At age 1 week, seen at a home visit by the pediatrician, she was eating and sleeping well. When awake she was alert and responsive to her environment. She was described as a fair-skinned baby with blue eyes, silky hair, and a pug nose.

For about a month after Joan's birth there was relative peace between Mr. and Mrs. O'Neal, and he came often to see the baby. Shortly thereafter, in a rage at finding her door locked in the middle of the night, he kicked it down. Following this episode she bought a gun but did not for long avoid being with Mr. O'Neal. At no time were we given an opportunity to work with him, though several of the staff met him. From the beginning Mrs. O'Neal presented the situation as one in which separation and her plan for divorce meant that only she and her baby would be involved in the study. Alarmed at Mr. O'Neal's violence in what was seen as a potential for tragedy involving them all, Mrs. O'Neal's social worker tried to help her realize the seriousness of Mr. O'Neal's recurrent rages and the danger of her own behavior. It became clear, however, that she could not free herself of him, for reasons we were to understand better as we worked with her. It became apparent that the fighting, excitement, and danger were necessary to Mrs. O'Neal. When the excitement of fighting with him was absent for very long, she became depressed and sought conflict elsewhere. She spoke with particular relish about her verbal battles. The stormy and dangerous relationship with Mr. O'Neal continued until Joan was almost 2 years old and included periods when Mrs. O'Neal left Joan with her father as a baby-sitter. There was no evidence that our warnings about potential danger to the baby influenced Mrs. O'Neal. When the relationship between them ended, it was, it appeared to us, not because she was at last convinced of its danger and destructiveness but because, as will be seen, she no longer had psychological need of Mr. O'Neal.

The foregoing account of Mrs. O'Neal's history and behavior contains the relevant data that emerged as we tried to make psychological sense of her stormy life in order to be of help to her and her child. Some of our understanding of Mrs. O'Neal was based on what we learned only in the closing months of the study, as is characteristic of therapeutic relationships over time. Although information about Mrs. O'Neal's own nurturing before she was 3 years old was sparse, it seems likely that it was far from optimal in view of the chronicity of her strongly aggressive behavior after the temporary separation from home at age 3. In addition were the unpredictable explosive outbursts of her father and the unprotective passivity of her mother. Her fear of her father led her in the direction of an identification with the aggressor. But her relationship with her father was complex: He not only was explosive and frightening but offered some of the libidinal supplies missing in her relationship with her mother. Her love for her father, her longing for him, her fear of him, and her bitter disappointment at what she experienced as his thwarting of her oedipal wishes, all combined in a love-hate struggle of particular intensity. The fighting that became characteristic of the father-daughter relationship was tinged with both counterphobic and erotic elements.

An Attempt to Understand

Overdetermining the direction of Mrs. O'Neal's identification with
her father was the parental preference for a boy. In response, she
became what she thought her father wanted: boyish, tough, fearless,
aggressive. But in her disappointment and anger at still not pleasing
him, much of her aggression was directed at him. Mrs. O'Neal's
hostility toward her mother was almost totally unconscious, possibly
because to acknowledge it would have risked loss of the relationship.
But the ways in which Mrs. O'Neal expressed anger from at least
age 5 on were equally punishing of both parents. From the beginning, her school career was a painful affront to her parents, because
of both her behavior problems and her embarrassing mediocrity as
a student despite her obvious intellectual ability. The anger Mrs.
O'Neal felt toward her parents was manifested partly in her early
and continuing hostility to teachers, patently displaced from her
education-valuing parents. At age 21 she still expressed an almost
consuming hatred of her first-grade teacher and a dislike of all subsequent teachers.

Moving out of her parent's home, she lived in a way that further
humiliated them: supported by public welfare in an inner city, involving herself in an interracial marriage to a man who was nearly
illiterate. Characteristic of the adult Mrs. O'Neal became were moods
alternating from a manic sense of her own omnipotence to a depression in which very low self-esteem was manifested in masochism,
impulsive self-destructive behavior, and marked deterioration in personal appearance. Her feelings of omnipotence allowed her initially
to believe that she could rescue Mr. O'Neal from his past; at the
same time her masochistic impulses allowed her to make a choice
that was humiliating to her. When danger from Mr. O'Neal was
apparent, her need to be fearless and tough operated as well as self-
destructive flirting with death, revealed at times in obsessive thoughts,
especially about violent death. Her experience with Mr. O'Neal re-
capitulated at a level of greater danger the stormy course of her relationship to her father. Out of years of risking what she considered
the potential violence of her father, she was virtually addicted to the

excitement and danger of conflict with Mr. O'Neal. It was as if life with him was a way of having her father. Exposing herself to danger also provided a way to counteract her depression and perhaps to appease to some extent her guilt over what she had done to her parents. In addition, it is likely that her choice of Mr. O'Neal was determined by positive aspects of her identification with her father since his profession required that he epitomize freedom from racial bias and work actively to help young men of minority groups. Their daughter's relationship to Mr. O'Neal presented her parents with a diabolic and exquisitely painful dilemma. How could they oppose the very ideas they had always supported? Whatever their private feelings, they reacted to the initial visits their daughter made to their home with Mr. O'Neal only as manifestations of her humanitarian wish to be helpful to a deprived young man. When she announced her intention to marry him, instead of the blowup that she expected, both parents reacted with stunned passivity and put their efforts not into opposition but into trying to keep Mr. O'Neal's racial identity a secret from their friends and professional colleagues. Later Mrs. O'Neal was to discuss her father's failure to oppose the marriage as a disappointment and a way in which he had failed her.

Functioning as a Mother

As a mother Mrs. O'Neal used the project well. The major threat to Joan's good development was her mother's inability for the first two years to protect the child from the violent, stormy, sadomasochistic scenes between her parents. (The child was never physically abused by either parent, as far as we know.) The mother's failure to protect Joan was not, as we see it, due to failing to value her. Rather, except in relation to Mr. O'Neal, she was fiercely protective, saw Joan as having the characteristics she was proud of in herself, spoke of her as a super child in a way that was reminiscent of her almost manic characteristics when she appeared to feel powerful and omniscient. We saw no evidence of negative feelings or behavior toward Joan that were unmistakably related to the child's appearance, although very early in her life her mother frequently asked whether or not her blue eyes would change, revealing possibly some concern about mixed racial characteristics. Joan was described by observers from a year onward as "a fair-skinned little girl, with slightly negroid features, blue eyes, and dark brown curly hair frequently worn in an Afro style." This description conveys the way Joan still appeared to others at age 8½ when seen during the follow-up study. The affect attached to the mother's periodic questions about changes of eye and skin color probably shifted over time, at first reflecting Mrs. O'Neal's anticipated dismay should a dramatic change occur. While we cannot be sure of her precise feelings at various times about Joan's appearance, what is important in the context of her functioning as Joan's mother was that her major problem in the maternal role was predictable on the basis of her longstanding personality characteristics. No evidence developed that feelings about racial issues were centrally involved in her relationship with her child.

Mrs. O'Neal's good use of the project services as a mother may have been determined partly by a wish to reproach her parents through finding us "better parents." There were a few instances in which she reported advice from her mother about child care contrary to ours and enjoyed being able to tell her mother she was wrong. There was also, however, in Mrs. O'Neal a great need for the acceptance and approval she had so seldom experienced. In view of her tendency to create conflict, to be belligerent, challenging, and scornful, especially to people in authority, it is noteworthy that almost without exception her demeanor with project staff was appropriate and friendly. She seemed to hunger for contact, in most things wanted our approval, attempted to prolong her visits with family team members, and had many appropriate and acceptable ways of doing so. She asked very good questions about both child health and general child care. She took a lively interest in Joan's developmental progress. Two months after the baby's birth the developmental examiner recorded: "Mrs. O'Neal is likable, observant, thoughtful, able to give good descriptions of the baby's reactions." Reflecting the genuine feeling of trust she developed in the pediatrician Mrs. O'Neal said, "She knows absolutely everything about babies."

The child care issues that came up during the first nine months of

Joan's life were not major ones and Mrs. O'Neal responded well to suggestions made to her. For example, around 5 months it was noted that she was overfeeding Joan as well as herself, but she was able, as some of the project mothers were not, to follow the pediatrician's advice about reducing the baby's caloric intake. At 8 months she brought up a question about toilet training and though there was much evidence that she was disgusted by diaper changing, she followed advice to postpone attempts at training. Similarly, she was repelled by Joan's messing in food but did allow the finger feeding that was suggested.

Very early we had predicted that Mrs. O'Neal would be able to tolerate the dependence of the early months but would begin to have trouble as the baby walked and moved toward greater autonomy and assertiveness. This proved to be a correct prediction. The first sign of this difficulty came in Joan's seventh month, when Mrs. O'Neal was very reluctant to allow her out of the playpen. Then at 10 months, as Joan did things her mother abhorred, like picking up a cracker from the floor and eating it, her sudden loud "no's" frightened Joan. It was difficult for Mrs. O'Neal to respond simply by diverting Joan or picking her up. Also it was noted that she had begun to attribute to Joan the intent to be destructive in the most innocent of activities. Mrs. O'Neal's intelligence and her undoubted valuing of her child did not help her realize the child's inability, at the age of 9 months, to anticipate what would happen when, for example, she picked up a book by one leaf and it tore; Mrs. O'Neal assumed that Joan was being deliberately naughty.

Joan's Development

When Mrs. O'Neal again enrolled in college, Joan, then 9 months, made the adjustment to daycare with little apparent distress beyond crying briefly each day for several weeks at the moment her mother left the center. For the next three months, however, her progress in development was less favorable than earlier, reflecting periods of heightened tension at home and her mother's preoccupation with her own feelings. However, Joan was a resilient baby who quickly recovered when corrective measures were introduced. On her 12-month developmental evaluation she functioned well in all areas measured by the test and her qualitative performance was also very good. A sturdy, active, healthy-looking child, Joan walked unassisted and could climb into an adult chair. Hand and finger skills were well developed. Motor activities were well modulated for her age. Wary in the beginning, she later became friendly and responsive, exchanging toys and smiles and enjoying the contact with the examiner, most of it from the safety of her mother's lap. Her attention to and insight regarding the test materials were excellent. For example, she found a toy hidden behind the solid screen, reflecting both her memory of it and the initiative and motivation to recover it. Her preferences were strong and unmistakable. Her liveliness, animation, and the interesting changes in facial expression added to her attractiveness. During the course of the session, affective expression included happy chortling, vocalizing with quiet pleasure, a look of perplexity when given a particular toy, fussing in a slightly anxious way to get to her mother, and angry, vehement fussing when her activity was interfered with. She had a three-word vocabulary, was beginning to use jargon, and recognized the names of several objects, actions, and persons.

At age 14 months Joan was described by a daycare staff member as follows: "Her most salient characteristics are her grace, her pleasant, quiet, relaxed air of self-sufficiency as she plays contentedly." She was also described as doing many things well; she concentrated to see how toys worked, enjoyed her play, and was a cooperative, amiable toddler. But at around 15 months Mrs. O'Neal's overreaction to Joan's emerging assertiveness was resulting in some mutual expressions of anger, with Mrs. O'Neal suddenly shouting "no" to Joan and slapping her hands and with Joan also saying "no" and slapping back. There was never any evidence of physical punishment of Joan other than the hand slapping. It was Mrs. O'Neal's sudden explosive verbal outbursts more than the hitting that characterized her reactions to what she considered Joan's misbehavior. When she thought that Joan was behaving aggressively toward her, the child's behavior was totally unacceptable and needed to be suppressed. Yet she expected Joan in relation to others ". . . to be tough, to defend herself, to hit back harder than she is hit." When Mrs. O'Neal brought up Joan's hitting and defiant no's as a problem, she could understand intellectually Joan's inevitable confusion. She recognized that the child was required to suppress aggression toward her mother yet expected to be aggressive with others. But this was the area of child care in which Mrs. O'Neal was least influenced at this time either by discussion of why Joan was hitting or by suggestions of alternative ways of responding to the child's expressions of anger. At age 2, when Joan could talk well enough to do so, she succinctly expressed her confusion about her mother's expectations: playing with a mother doll and baby she said firmly, looking at the baby doll, "She's a bad girl!" Then she looked questioningly at a staff member and asked, "She's a good girl?"

By 16 months Joan was not doing as well in daycare as she had been two months earlier. She had become impatient, whiny, and difficult to comfort or divert. She reacted on some days with unprovoked anger, kicking and biting both staff and other children. On other days she was gentle and even loving, but her mood, which was apparent when she arrived each morning, lasted through the day. While, to be sure, some of the sharp contrasts in behavior and the ambivalent attitudes are to be expected in children of her age, in Joan they were exaggerated. Some of the fighting behavior seemed related to the mother's handling of any show of aggression in her, but it was quite likely even more responsive to her mother's withdrawal of interest from her at this time as she put great energy into a cause she espoused. This must have made her seem very different to her child since Mrs. O'Neal was less attentive, much more irritable and impatient in her behavior. When the changes in Joan and their probable cause were discussed with her she denied that Joan was missing her mother's usual devoted care, said Joan was "tough and could take it." At the 18-month developmental evaluation there was no deterioration of Joan's functioning on quantitative measures of the test, but it was noted that she was quite persistently negativistic and uncooperative in many ways and that her frustration tolerance was minimal.

The cause absorbing Mrs. O'Neal's energy was her almost single-handed attempt to save the project, and in particular daycare, from ending because of lack of funds. In her efforts she showed not only intelligence, resourcefulness, and persistence, but also her characteristic belligerence and grandiosity. Alliances with other parents in this attempt were quickly made and quickly broken as she would become angry in some disagreement. The threat of the loss of daycare brought about the only instance in which she allowed her anger to be obviously directed at project personnel. She was both our champion and our accuser. Our "wonderful service" had to be saved, but how dared we abandon her and her child! Fortunately, the crisis was averted, though not as a result of Mrs. O'Neal's efforts, and the care continued as long as she needed it. Nevertheless, some of the results of both the mother's inappropriate handling of Joan's assertiveness and her relative withdrawal from her were still seen at 19 months, when Joan's caregiver recorded the following: "Joan's language, motor skills, and problem solving are coming along well. However, controlling and appropriately expressing her anger and impatience are hard for her and often take away her ability to do the things we know she can do. She has developed a healthy independence which she overasserts at times but usually uses to help herself."

Joan, as before, had the capacity to respond quickly when her mother was again available to her, and by the time of her 24-month developmental evaluation she was friendly, cooperative, enthusiastic, and relaxed. She could express her protest and anger in acceptable ways.

Working on the Past and Moving Ahead

It was clear that Mrs. O'Neal's problems with aggression and her sadomasochistic attitudes and behavior had impinged less on her child than might have been expected from their vividness and prominence in her own history. It was fortunate that Mrs. O'Neal's valuing her child and her wish for staff approval helped her to use child-

care suggestions and advice more often than not. Of equal importance in outcome, however, was the change brought about especially
in her relationship to her father. A tremendous advantage in the
work with her about her father was his gentle and considerate reaction to Joan. Viewing Joan as part of herself contributed to Mrs.
O'Neal's seeing her father's tolerant, patient behavior with Joan almost as if it was with her. In her social work interviews, she could
then consider the possibility that she and her father had once been
close. She began reporting some memories to support this and sought
confirmation from her mother. Being sent away at age 3 and feeling
replaced by her sister in her father's affection were discussed during
her appointments as contributing to the anger that so powerfully
affected her subsequent relationship to her parents. She came to see
that she had developed early in life a pattern of approaching her
father antagonistically and thus getting not the love she so much
wanted but his frightening anger. Recognizing her own part in the
conflict with her father, she believed that since she had brought about
her father's reactions to her over the years, she could do so again but
with the possibility now of eliciting the kind of response she wanted.

Many aspects of identification with her father, her anger at her
mother, how these factors affected her personality, her school life,
and her marital choice were never fully explored since Mrs. O'Neal
was not ready to do so. Weekend visits with her parents provided
opportunity to use what she was learning about herself, to experi-
ment with new ways of behaving. The results were extremely gratifying to her, and motivation to look more closely into herself diminished sharply. It was as if she had never had it so good and didn't
want, as she said, to rock the boat.

Although working well on some problems and obviously beginning to function better with her parents, Mrs. O'Neal continued to
avoid any mention of Mr. O'Neal in spite of his irregular but continuing presence in her life. In retrospect, it may not be too improbable
to believe she knew, not intellectually but in some part of her, that
working directly on her involvement with him was not necessary,
that when she worked out her problems with her father she would

be psychologically free of Mr. O'Neal. Certainly her behavior was consistent with that idea when another episode of his violence occurred when Joan was 21 months old. Once more he broke into Mrs. O'Neal's apartment in the middle of the night, this time by smashing a window. In a drunken rage he broke up furniture and threw things at her. He made so much noise that Joan awakened and screamed in terror. Although the likelihood of the child's being frightened in the previous similar circumstances had been forcefully brought to Mrs. O'Neal's attention, she had never before acted on that knowledge. Our speculation is that she could so do now because of progress in improving greatly the relationship that was still the most important in her life—that to her father. She no longer needed Mr. O'Neal. She and Joan moved immediately into her parents' home. Such a step could have represented a shift back to carrying on her long-standing conflict directly with her father. Going home could have represented not progress but a regression. There is evidence to the contrary, however, based not only on Mrs. O'Neal's response to psychological intervention but on events in the five years of her life after the study ended. It was probably fortunate that the grandparents perceived Joan as a child who could "pass" in a white society. Their acceptance of her contributed in an important way to improving Mrs. O'Neal's relationship with her parents. Had they rejected Joan, our work with Mrs. O'Neal would have been much more difficult. Whether her choice of an Afro hairstyle for Joan was a remnant of her defiant attitude toward her parents or a wish not to deprive her child of part of her racial heritage, or both, remains a question.

Mrs. O'Neal's wish not to "rock the boat" left largely unexplored the area of her relationship with her mother. One facet of their relationship especially prominent after Mrs. O'Neal returned to live with her parents was very protective behavior toward her mother, especially in relieving her of a great deal of housework and yard work, thus being both a good daughter and a good son. The protective behavior seemed to be related to repressed anger at her mother, to guilt over the pain her marriage and other failures had caused, and to guilt over her success at last in winning her father's favor. However, her behavior was adaptive: It improved the psychological environment in which she and Joan lived, it pleased both parents, and it gave her a feeling of accomplishment as well.

After the move, distance from the center made it impractical for Joan to continue in daycare, but Mrs. O'Neal conscientiously kept all appointments with family team members, including Joan's last developmental evaluation at 30 months. Her pediatrician, who was observing the evaluation, reported the following: "Joan is a very competent little girl. She seems older than her 2½ years both in her accomplishments, and in her attitude toward the test situation, especially in her ability to follow instructions, concentrate, and persist at long tasks."

After Mrs. O'Neal and Joan had lived with the grandparents for five months, Mrs. O'Neal found employment that required her to live in another community. She made the move without hesitation but continued regular visits with her parents. As the project closed she was self-supporting and had a job of which she was proud. Her improved self-esteem was reflected in more careful dress and grooming, and she was pleased both with herself and with her child.

Follow-up

When seen in the follow-up study five years later, Joan, then age 7½, scored on testing well within the average range. She seemed to be invested in learning and had solid problem-solving skills. However, there was a marked contrast between her demeanor during testing and before and after it. During the testing, she was sober, quiet, serious, showed minimal pleasure over successes and anxiety over failures. She seemed socially uncomfortable with both the examiner and her mother during the testing. When not being tested, she spoke spontaneously and pleasantly to both. Her constraint and anxiety appeared to be directly related to testing. Her mother had chosen to send her to a school with overly high expectations of children both in behavior and achievement and in which the atmosphere is one of repression. This decision perhaps reflected Mrs. O'Neal's wish to ensure both her daughter's academic achievement and conforming behavior.

In Mrs. O'Neal's interview at follow-up she reported being pleased with Joan. She wished only that she was a little less sensitive but felt that made her nicely perceptive also. The same old wish for Joan to be tough enough to defend herself was revealed as well as a kind of companionable quality in their relationship. Joan was still the only child. Mrs. O'Neal had not remarried. She was again in college, receiving some financial help from her parents. She had made a career choice appropriate to her ability and compatible with her parents' values, having now made peace with them. She and Joan continued to live apart from the grandparents but visited them regularly. Mrs. O'Neal said that her mother wanted her not to let Joan know "she is a mulatto," but added that she made pictures of Joan's father available to her and anticipated that in the future she would want to know a great deal about him. Mrs. O'Neal's plan was to be honest about who he was but to put their separation only on the basis that they couldn't get along. Our impression at follow-up was that both mother and child were doing reasonably well and in some respects very well. We anticipated that the next few years would go smoothly for them since Mrs. O'Neal had made such gains in the ways she was able to function in her daily life, most importantly in modifying the tendency toward sadomasochistic interaction with people psychologically important to her and in considerably alleviating her self-defeating behavior. She was both less omnipotent in some of her behavior and more self-respecting. Obviously we do not suggest that we helped Mrs. O'Neal to solve all her psychological problems. However, there is no doubt about her improved adaptation and sense of well-being. It seems probable that Joan's adolescence will be more of a problem for her and her mother than is usual. The reasons for this expectation are apparent in the material reported.

PART III EVALUATION AND IMPLICATIONS

CHAPTER 9

Results of
Intervention

The case examples provide a clinical view of the project's results and the influence that participation in the project had on the individual mothers and children. The five cases were selected to represent the range of responses to intervention, and we comment further on each case now as a measure of results, believing that clinical assessments are as valid in their way as the quantitative data to be reported later.

Miss Galer, relatively healthy psychologically and with strong motivation to become self-supporting, needed and could use all services well. Medical care for Steven, her very sick infant, was crucial. Without the vigilance of her child's pediatrician, who was available at any hour needed, he could well have died. Without daycare Miss Galer would have had great trouble finding any plan for Steven's care at all comparable in quality. Her own standards would not have permitted her to place him just anywhere, and thus her own training and employment might have been greatly delayed, something she would have found hard to tolerate. The case material has also illustrated the ways in which the developmental assessments enabled her and the staff to safeguard Steven's development, as well as demonstrated that she needed and could use psychological support and help with emotional problems during an exceptionally stressful period of her life. In comparison with those of Mrs. Ives, Miss Keeler, and Mrs. O'Neal, her problems were much less serious, but interviews offered her a chance to make good use of her capacity for insight, helping her to manage her life and its relationships with less conflict. Thus much of the work with Miss Galer became a psychotherapeutic contact in which some of the burdens of her neurotic mechanisms were lightened.

139

Mrs. Ives, because of her severe psychological handicap, had tremendous need for support during the problem-laden first year of her child's life even though the infant Carrie was healthy and tolerant. During that period Mrs. Ives used the pediatrician and social worker almost to the limits of their physical and psychological energy. And daycare when Carrie's development was seriously at risk was a much needed resource. There was little need for sick baby care, but its availability was reassuring to this highly anxious mother. Mrs. Ives's fragile psychological state placed sharp limitations on her potential for change in functioning. However, she was able to use a narrow range of supportive services at a time when she and her child most needed them.

Mrs. Madison's essentially healthy personality allowed her to make good use of the project services related to the care of Paul, an infant who had special needs for several months. While her use of available services was rather circumscribed, her response to the help she needed most acutely was excellent. We had originally accepted her for admission to the study because of concern about her health and that of the coming baby but also because of concern over how Mr. Madison's leaving her would affect her and the care of her baby. There was little direct attention to the latter aspect of the situation during the work with Mrs. Madison because the difficulties of caring for Paul overshadowed everything else. But at follow-up five years after the project ended we learned that we had been right to be concerned about the loss of her husband because she had been much more upset about that than she could express during admission interviews, and the support of the staff, she felt, had helped to lessen her feelings of loss and abandonment. She also found much reassurance in the results of the developmental evaluations, having feared that her child's physical problems might cause delay in his overall development.

Miss Keeler's response to intervention efforts was very limited, in contrast to that of Mrs. Madison. Because of the personality damage and constriction she had sustained in her own growing up, she could respond to very little of what was available to her. While she, too, made use of the help she was aware of needing, it was unfortunately limited, as far as we could tell, to little more than medical care for her child, Greg, help with her own health and anxiety about it, and help with housing. While one of our usual purposes was to assist parents to achieve their own goals, in this instance we tried to modify the mother's goals with respect to the kind of child she wanted because her restrictiveness, severity, and insensitivity to his needs deprived him, we believed, of some of his developmental potential. As a result, a promising child is no longer so promising though he and his mother seem quite satisfied with each other. We chose to include this family in our selections because there are many like it in our society. Those who plan and carry out intervention programs and especially those who finance them should be aware that though many, if not most, disadvantaged families can be helped substantially, some can be helped only in limited ways that still are important to them and are well worth supporting.

While for Mrs. O'Neal the pediatric care, child care counseling, developmental assessment, and availability of daycare were all important and reasonably well used, of special importance in her life and Joan's was the opportunity to work through some of her more severe psychological problems. Although quite disturbed, Mrs. O'Neal was able to make significant progress in modifying some of her more maladaptive and self-destructive behaviors; there were, however, some problems that could not be addressed.

It would make an excessively long report to describe all the families and their use of services, but we believe each benefited in some degree, two, along with Miss Keeler, marginally. One of these was a young woman who had less need for our services than was at first assumed; she was minimally involved, sending the child with her grandmother for physical exams and developmental evaluations and only occasionally talking with the social worker about herself and her child, sometimes only by telephone. The other was a young woman who made good use of medical care, daycare, and help with vocational training and employment but had a deep-seated neurotic problem to which we had little access and which would have required intensive therapy to change. The case material strongly suggested that for her, her son was psychologically the child of her father. She and the child lived with her parents the first two years of his life, until the parents urged her to move into an apartment of her own. It was then that she began to deteriorate in general functioning, in care of her child, and in self-care. Shortly after the close of the project she left her job, lived on welfare, and at follow-up was still on welfare, having moved to another state. By the time he was 8, the child had been living with his grandparents for a year, visiting his mother occasionally. When seen at follow-up the grandmother, displeased with her daughter, said she gave Children's House the credit for the boy's good development.

Utilization of services was analyzed. Each service available was used to some extent by all but one participant, whose child was in neither daycare nor toddler school. The list below shows the percentage of families using the services to either *moderate* or *major* degrees:

Service	*Percentage of Families*
Medical Care	88
Daycare and/or Toddler School	76
Psychological Support or Counseling	65
Tangible Services Other than Medical Care or Daycare/Toddler School	53
Child Care Counseling	41
Abstract Child Development Information	13

Reflected in these figures is what parents felt most in need of and could best use. That is, medical care, daycare or toddler school, and psychological services were most extensively used. In contrast, while not unimportant, abstract child development information was much less utilized. Extent of use says nothing about qualitative aspects, about how much families benefited from such use. As in the examples given, the individual case records reveal differences in the extent to which families benefited through participation in the program and in what ways they benefited.

We now present data based on findings pertaining to all of the study children and their mothers as a group, referred to from here on as the intervention group. Information about fathers is not included because of its relatively fragmentary nature. The results are derived from four sources: observations of the advanced social, emotional, and play behavior of the children between the ages of 24 and 30 months; a comparison group study made when the children were 30 months old; and two interrelated follow-up studies done five years after the project ended, when the children in the intervention group were between 7½ and 8 years.

It came as something of a surprise to us that the children 24 to 30 months old were able to understand and use the concepts of sharing and of ownership to the extent they did. They not only imitated staff behavior in being helpful to one another but also seemed to identify with staff behavior and feelings in their concern for each other and their ability to give some degree of comfort, including comforting words. They engaged in interactions requiring the ability to be aware of simple cause and effect sequences and to use fairly complex mediating processes. They sought play companions in various ways, including verbally. At times some were able to play in a genuinely cooperative way for brief periods. Their ability to engage in imaginative play was well beyond what had been anticipated from the literature on children their age. Their teasing and behavior in conflict situations revealed the use of surprisingly sophisticated strategies, often making use of full awareness of the feelings and preferences of another child in a particular context. Several formed attachments to another child that lasted not briefly but over the life of the project. (Not all the children developed each capacity to the same degree or at the same age, and each child's state from both day to day and hour to hour affected his competence in these areas.) Illustrative examples are given in Appendix 1.

A comparison group of eighteen children 30 months of age who were not in the project was selected from the same hospital clinic as the intervention group. Families were matched on the basis of income, marital status of the mother, and race of parents. Children were matched on sex and ordinal position. All were full-term and free from congenital defect and neonatal illness. Each comparison-group child was seen once for developmental evaluation by a psychologist not involved in the intervention project. Results were compared with evaluations of the intervention children at 30 months using the same instrument, the Yale Developmental Schedules. Various analyses of the resulting data are given in the first of the two papers referred to in Chapter 1 (Rescorla, Provence, and Naylor 1982). Here we report only the following from the comparison group study: There was a definite but not statistically significant superiority of the intervention group over the comparison group in total developmental quotient (105.3 versus 98.1) and in adaptive developmental quotient (106.5 versus 101.5). There was a significant difference in language developmental quotient, with the intervention group children scoring 99.4 and the comparison group scoring 85.5. The superior language function of the intervention group was in both vocabulary and syntactic development.

On total developmental quotient, sixteen of the intervention group scored between 95 and 132, one between 80 and 95, and one below 80. In the comparison group twelve children scored between 95 and 130, five between 80 and 95, and one below 80. The median for the intervention group was 105.5 and for the comparison group, 99.5. In the adaptive (problem-solving) area, fifteen of the intervention group were between 95 and 143, two were between 80 and 95, and one was below 80. In the comparison group, ten scored between 95 and 128, seven between 80 and 95, and one below 80. The median for the intervention group was 105.5, and for the comparison group, 98.5. In the language area sixteen of the eighteen children in the intervention group scored between 95 and 139 and two below 80. In the comparison group four children scored between 95 and 132, eight children between 80 and 95, and six below 80. The median language score in the intervention group was 101, and in the comparison group, 81.

Of the two interrelated follow-up studies five years after the close of the program, one was an independent study conducted by Trickett, Apfel, Rosenbaum, and Zigler (1982); the other was conducted by the Child Study Center staff and included an interview of the mother by her social worker or her child's pediatrician and tests of the child (Wechsler Intelligence Scale for Children—Revised, Draw-A-Person, and Beery Test of Visual Motor Integration) by a psychologist who did not know the families. Data analysis was done by a second psychologist not involved in the project. Data from I.Q. testing (the WISC-R, DAP, and VMI) showed that the intervention children continued to function somewhat above the norm for inner-city disadvantaged children (average score 91.8). The pattern of verbal and performance scores suggested that strengths in language function had persisted in the intervention group compared with what is often found in disadvantaged samples (Consortium for Longitudinal Studies 1978).

The Trickett study employed two comparison groups: one from an impoverished neighborhood where most of the intervention families lived at the start of the project and a second from a slightly less impoverished neighborhood where the next largest proportion of intervention families lived at the start of the project. Schools for control-group selection were chosen from each neighborhood on the basis of having populations representative of the neighborhood. This study consisted of interviews with intervention and comparison-group mothers, mainly for demographic information, testing of children at school, and collection of data from school records regarding attendance, grade placement, and grades. The comparison group from the slightly less impoverished neighborhood is referred to as Group I; the one from the more impoverished neighborhood, as Group II.

The major findings of the Trickett study on the children are these: For both boys and girls in the intervention group, school attendance was better than for either control group. On the Peabody Picture Vocabulary Test the mean score for the intervention group was significantly above that for both control groups. On the Peabody Individual Achievement Test, the intervention-group children and control Group I (the less disadvantaged group) functioned on the average at age level while Group II was well below age level. On both tests, the mean for the girls in the intervention group was significantly higher than the mean for both control groups whereas the mean for boys was similar to that for control Group I but significantly better than the mean for control Group II.

The parent interviews in the Child Study Center follow-up covered changes in family unit, residence, education, and occupation, and elicited the parent's opinion of the child's general development and school experiences. Parents were also asked for an appraisal of the project and a description of their child. The most striking findings pertained to the upward mobility of the intervention families. They made remarkable gains by several indices of upward mobility in comparison with their status at the start of the project. Ten of the seventeen mothers made advances in education during the life of the project, and at follow-up eight had obtained additional education. Three had gained no additional education in either period. Progress toward economic self-sufficiency was also evident. The number of families on welfare by the end of the project had declined from nine to five; at follow-up only two were still on welfare. In addition, birth rate in the families seems to have been strongly influenced by the project, though at no time was there intention to exert such an influence. Fourteen families had only one child at the end of the project; ten of the seventeen still had only one child five years later.

An attempt was made to assess general improvement in quality of life for the intervention families. At the end of the project, when the children were 30 months old, quality of life had improved for twelve families, judged by positive change in one or more of the following areas: housing, medical care of the parent, educational or training status, socioeconomic status, social life, or engagement in community life. Judged by the same criteria at follow-up five years later, fourteen families gave evidence of improvement in two or more ways. Two who were not materially better off seemed happier in their personal life and more positive in outlook. One mother, as indicated earlier, had deteriorated in quality of life and general functioning. Findings of the independent study based on data concerning both the intervention and control-group parents are compatible with those reported above. Trickett et al. (1982) state: "The parents changed dramatically as a result of their involvement in this program. In addition to having moved to somewhat better neighborhoods, the intervention mothers, as compared to their controls, had smaller families, were more frequently employed and had a higher socioeconomic status" (p. 219).

An additional kind of information compiled in the Child Study Center follow-up cannot be considered "hard" research data. We are aware that "customer satisfaction" is not usually accepted as evidence that intervention goals have been accomplished. Whether or not those involved in a program feel they are helped, however, does seem to us relevant, and their opinion about what services they value is an important part of the planning and delivery of health and social services. Such information was gathered as interviewers asked mothers for their appraisal of the program, explaining that we needed their frank opinion rather than polite answers because of the possible effect their responses could have on services for other young parents and children. Our records contain the exact response of each mother, but, in summary, all responses were strongly positive, not only to the Child Study Center staff but also to the independent investigators. The following is quoted from a Trickett study working paper: "All 17 mothers rated the overall program as 'very helpful,' the highest rating. . . . Most were able to name specific positive features of each aspect of the program. This ability to provide convincing, detailed backup for their positive ratings convinces us that most of these mothers did indeed view the program with very positive feelings. The fact that they continued to hold these views five years after the program had ended is further evidence of the impressive impact this program must have had on their lives."*

Interviews by Child Study Center staff with parents reflected variation in what they valued most, but all components of the program were mentioned as helpful. Examples of the most all-encompassing statements were these: "I would never have survived those early difficult times without you," from the mother of a very jittery, uncomfortable, crying baby. "It was the best thing that ever happened to me," from a depressed young mother. "It was the luckiest thing in our lives," from parents who abused their infant and

---

* Personal communication.

needed much help in controlling their dangerous impulses. One mother spoke of how much the program had helped her and added that she used what she learned in dealing with her second child. Several spoke of missing the contact with the social worker after the program closed. One stressed how much her child's learning ability had been promoted. One said that the developmental evaluations were reassuring as prevention, adding that by the time an ordinary mother knew something was wrong with her child it was already too late. This came from a woman whose schooling had stopped at the tenth grade but who had obviously continued to learn. Another said that after learning what daycare could be, she would advise a mother not to place her child in just any center but to be particular. Several parents spoke wistfully of missing the kind of daycare and medical care provided their child. One, a young woman we came to know as functionally retarded, said it had helped her to have someone she could talk to about problems because it wasn't good to hold them inside. Another commented that her social worker made it possible for her to look at alternatives and not rush into bad decisions. Still another mother said, "The medical care was excellent and gave me confidence in my own judgment. The developmental evaluations were exciting." She added, "It did a lot for me to have the contact with the social worker. My mother was critical of the project for too much psychology, but I found your way of understanding behavior, my own and the children's, helpful." This same mother and two others said the only negative thing they could think of was that the project ended too soon and they had not been able to find comparable services elsewhere.

Parent comments were also strongly positive about their child's personality and development with just enough acknowledgment of a problem here and there to give their accounts credibility. Since many of each child's characteristics and interaction between parent and child were observed in the testing situation at follow-up, we have some objective evidence that the parents' favorable descriptions of their children were based on reality and reflected their positive feelings accurately.

CHAPTER 10

Retrospective Appraisal
and Conclusions

After completing the follow-up study we made an appraisal of the program as a whole, asking the following questions: Were we to undertake a similar intervention program, would the theoretical assumptions and methods be the same? If not, what would we change? Did we learn anything as the work progressed that would necessitate changes in or additions to planned procedures? Did certain phenomena emerge that can be seen most clearly in retrospect, suggesting unexpected influences that may have been as important in outcome as those that were carefully planned? What were the major determinants of the results? Can the services, methods, and results of this intervention program provide a reliable basis for the organization and delivery of effective services to other disadvantaged children and their parents? We tried to answer these questions as dispassionately as possible and share our answers here with the thought that they may be of use to others.

We found no reason to change the general theoretical approach as described in Chapter 3. In our experience it had practical as well as conceptual value, because the guidelines it offered could be used to develop not only the general plan of providing services but the basis for individualizing them according to the varying conditions and needs of each family. But certain aspects of practice deserve special emphasis because of their relationship to the course and outcome of this project and their relevance to the organization and delivery of effective services.

Aspects of Practice Influencing Outcome

The study has, in our view, borne out a number of assumptions about how to provide services. These important factors in providing service can be summarized as follows:

1. A competent staff is essential. To put it simply, persons providing services should know what they are doing. More will be said of this later.

2. It is both feasible and sound to combine in a service team clinicians, educators and child-care providers, professionals, and paraprofessionals. Each contributes something important to the whole both in providing specific services—preventive and therapeutic— and in adding to the effectiveness of the group effort. The whole, in this instance, is indeed more than the sum of its parts, since coordination of efforts prevents the wasteful fragmentation of services so common in current health and social-service delivery systems.

3. Providing services to both parents and children is more effective than providing services only to children with minimal participation of parents. This has two dimensions: Since the young child's development at any one point is always closely linked with his parent, immediate and short-range goals for enhancing development must be addressed to the parent-child relationship and interaction, with all this implies. But there is a long-range consideration as well: Improving the adaptive capacities of the parents, assisting them in their lives as adults as well as parents, exerts in most instances a positive influence on their functioning that continues into the future to the child's benefit. Similarly, supplementing parental care with direct services to the child has a demonstrably beneficial effect on the child's functioning. Thus we conclude that services to parents as well as to children are essential if one expects to assist disadvantaged families materially. Bronfenbrenner (1974), Gray and Wandersman (1980), and Heinicke and Strassman (1980) all have stressed the importance of providing services to parents in order to prevent the erosion of gains made by children in preschool programs. Such a conclusion acknowledges and emphasizes the complexity of human

development, one element being the influence of parent and child upon one another, in a complex interactional system—the family.

4. Time is an important dimension in more than one sense: For the parent, ample time in individual contacts to be heard and to hear and time to develop a sense of confidence in the staff and an awareness of what assistance is available; for the child, time to experience the continuity of benevolent interest, care, and education; for the staff, time to individualize services to families and to talk with colleagues in the coordination of effort. The importance of time is frequently overlooked as service providers strive to include as many persons as possible in their program.

5. Individualizing services is essential. The case examples illustrate the individual approaches required for effective work with specific parents and children. Not everyone needs or utilizes all components of a program in the same way or on the same timetable. Yet planners tend to assume a uniformity about the needs of "the poor" or "the disadvantaged" and their use of services. This assumption may result in poor practice. Individualizing services demands flexibility and resourcefulness of program and staff. It may be achieved only imperfectly, to be sure; there are limits to what one program or group can do. But it is clear that if individualization is not valued and planned for, it is unlikely to occur. Even arrangements made by those strongly motivated to deliver high-quality services have a tendency to become routinized and rigid unless they are continuously watched over to ensure that individual personality characteristics and varying, changing needs are recognized and considered.

THE RELEVANCE OF SUPPORT TO STAFF

While it was expected that psychological support would be provided for the staff, it proved to be even more important than anticipated, and we believe this would be true for other programs. Intensive work with disadvantaged families brings great satisfactions, but it is also difficult, physically and emotionally strenuous, and at times unrewarding. Staff support takes several forms: Intellectual stimulation is a must, not just for those who require further training but also for experienced, sophisticated professionals. Perhaps the most important factor in assuring the staff's ongoing development and effectiveness is an atmosphere of inquiry, of intellectual curiosity focused on efforts to understand behavior. But it is also important to respond promptly to staff members' distress about problems they are dealing with in parents or children. Just as essential is the development of a way of solving the inevitable problems among staff members that interfere with working together. The presence or absence of such supports strongly influences staff morale. We have written of this in detail elsewhere (Provence, Naylor, and Patterson 1977) and will emphasize here only the conviction that support for the staff is a vitally important dimension of such a group effort and requires planning and thoughtful attention.

THE RELEVANCE OF WORKING WITH PARENTS

There can be little doubt that changes in almost all parents were in the direction of improved capacity for adaptation. The role of the intervention program in improving the parents' adaptation can be described in accordance with current views of successful personal adaptation on an individual level. Coelho, Hamburg, and Adams (1974) point to three important components of successful adaptation: (1) the individual's capability and skill to deal with social and environmental demands, including coping abilities; (2) his motivation to interact with the environment; and (3) his capacity to maintain a state of psychological equilibrium so that energies can be directed to external needs. His adequacy in meeting adaptive tasks depends to a great extent on the support, guidance, and facilitation he receives from significant other persons and from society at large. In large measure his skills and psychological equilibrium depend on the adequacy of society's preparatory institutions (family, schools, etc.); motivation and the ability to maintain self-esteem under stressful conditions are closely related to successful adaptation and coping; the ability to maintain psychological comfort depends upon both intrapsychic resources and on the social supports available in the environment.

All parents in the project suffered to one degree or another from problems related to educational and social disadvantage. By enabling them to continue learning in several ways, the intervention services made up in part for some of the education deficits. For a group deprived of many of the social supports available to those who are more advantaged, the social supports provided through the study were of particular significance, not simply in their objective value, but in their psychological meaning. Medical care, daycare services, assistance in learning to negotiate the social system, help to reduce psychological stress—all were important.

Perhaps of preeminent importance were the relationships through which services were provided. The expectation that we would be trying to help a particularly needy group of young parents in a difficult period of their lives led to much emphasis on being aware of their needs. Some parents turned out to have more strengths than were at first recognized, but we are nevertheless left with the impression that for all of them the emphasis on giving to *them* in various ways contributed to their devotion to the study and to their tolerance for their children's receiving services and experiential enrichment that had not been part of their own lives. It may not be too fanciful to suggest that for most of the parents participation in the study became in part a corrective emotional experience, making up for some of the deficits in their early life experiences, supplying the caring "parents" some still needed, and for most providing opportunities to further their education and gain skills valued in the marketplace. Those who used the opportunity to increase their knowledge and skills began with some degree of motivation to improve their situation. But even strong motivation becomes more productive when there are both hope, based in part on a realistic view of one's capability and opportunity, and sufficient self-esteem to believe in the possibility of success. As described in Chapter 2, part of the work with parents was focused on learning what their goals for themselves were and on helping them to implement them. Probably of most importance was not suggesting strategies, though this was at times appropriate, but conveying confidence in the parent's potential for reaching goals, providing a reason for hope of success. The entire program in many ways contributed to heightened self-esteem, which in turn made its contribution to improved adaptive capacity.

The third major component of successful adaptation, the capacity to maintain a state of psychological equilibrium, suggests an optimal and perhaps relatively unattainable human condition, an absolute. However, when applied to the practical demands of daily life, including employment and child care, psychological equilibrium can be taken to mean the ability to leave internal demands temporarily in abeyance while meeting external demands. Clinical experience suggests that one's capacity for coping with the external environment is heightened as stresses from both inside and outside are reduced. Part of the work with parents in this study was directed at how they and we together could alleviate excessive stress from whatever source and thereby, it was assumed, increase coping capacity. As Mechanic (1974) suggests, coping capacities include the ability to control the demands to which the individual is exposed and the pace of those demands. Perhaps one example of improved coping is reflected in the decision of most of the parents to control the pace of increasing the size of their families—a decision that for many reflected a more general attitude of "planfulness" and hopefulness, more confidence and self-esteem than had characterized them earlier.

Of particular interest are the long-term effects of the intervention as seen in the superiority of the study children over the control children at age 7½ or 8 years on the measures used and the improvement in quality of life of most of the families; we propose that the work with the parents was an indispensable factor in the results. Trickett et al. (1982), as a result of the independent follow-up study, agree that "the key element in this intervention was the work done with the parents" (p. 218).

How might one understand the relationship between participation in the project and improved adaptive capacity in the mothers? Our hypothesis is that mothers changed markedly in their feelings of self-worth, that their relationships with project staff made a great difference in how they saw themselves as parents and as individuals. Improved self-esteem resulted from the overall atmosphere of the center, from the skill of all the staff and their benevolent interest in both parents and children, from contacts with social workers, teachers, pediatricians, developmental examiners, all of whom spent many hours with each parent. It was a first experience for parents, for example, to have professional people spend as much time with them as their questions and comments required. One parent expressed her pleasure in always having her questions responded to as worthy of serious consideration and commented that she had never been talked down to. As a result of innumerable interchanges with staff, parents could not have failed to feel valued and better about themselves than before. A certain amount of self-love is known to be necessary for development of the capacity to love, and perhaps that capacity was heightened a bit. We do not claim that without us the parents would not have valued themselves and hence their children. We do, however, suggest that their experiences in the study increased their sense of worth and that our valuing them as well as their children increased their native capacity to value their children.

We would suggest, further, that giving to and valuing the parents allowed them in varying degrees to identify with staff members' feelings and attitudes toward their children and that such identification had a beneficial effect. In that regard, psychoanalytic psychology holds that the identification process whereby an individual becomes like another person in some ways is a natural accompaniment of mental development and aids in the learning process. Nunberg (1932, 1955) commented that identification is the basis of mutual understanding and contact between people. A mother's ability to identify with her infant facilitates the nurturing and reciprocity. A developing child's identification with parents is an important factor in his learning. As Hartmann, Kris, and Loewenstein (1946) put it, he "participates in their reactions and thus acquires their methods of solving problems and coping with emergencies" (p. 47). Attitudes are taken over as well as modes of action and reaction. Kris (1948, 1975) has pointed out that every step in learning in childhood and many steps of learning in later life involve conscious and unconscious identifications. Identifications also play a role in the therapeutic work, both from the side of the therapist and from the side of the patient. The capacity for identification of each with the other facilitates communication. Identification with therapist or teacher is part of the process of

change and learning. And the therapist or teacher who cannot identify with the patient or pupil is unlikely to be effective in therapeutic
or educational efforts.

Mothers in the project came to hold some of the attitudes of those
who worked with them, sometimes with full awareness, sometimes
much more subtly. At times they asked for and accepted information
and recommendations about various aspects of infant care that appeared to be useful to them in the short run. At other times they
rejected or ignored suggestions. Nonetheless over a longer period
they appeared to incorporate attitudes that, in our view, were favorable for their children's development. To one degree or another and
at varying times, they took over attitudes and aspects of the behavior
of staff members toward their children. The result was that even
those who at times did not follow what we suggested as specific
child-rearing practices came to have, in the main, a certain kind of
feeling for their children. These attitudes may be more important to
a child's development than whether he is toilet trained too early or
is too severely punished for misbehavior.

Another abiding result of participation in the project was that parents became aware that a child's development proceeds in ways that
they can try to understand and can influence. They also learned that
when things are not going well and they are worried, there are ways
of seeking and insisting upon appropriate services. The follow-up
material illustrated these two points impressively.

The Question of Transferability

What then, do we see as the essential services for assisting disadvantaged parents and their young children, and can these services be
transferred to other settings?

One thing we urge upon others embarking on a similar effort is
to make as explicit as they can the assumptions and constructs that
guide their practice. Whether they agree with the constructs presented in Chapter 3 matters less than that clinicians and educators
engaged in such applications of knowledge try to be as clear as pos-

sible about the concepts and experiences that substantively influence their work.

We also emphasize the indispensability of knowledge from the mental health field in developing programs to assist disadvantaged families. It is well known, and has been illustrated in this project, that many of those persons called disadvantaged are characterized by maladaptive behavior or crippling personality problems from a variety of causes. It is also a fact that most of the mental health and developmental problems of infants and young children, whether disadvantaged or not, are dealt with by parents and by workers who are not mental health professionals. Clearly, as Cohen and his colleagues (1975) emphasize, if one is committed to the importance of early recognition and alleviation of developmental and mental health problems, "the body of knowledge derived from theories and practices of psychiatry, social work and clinical psychology must find its way more fully and effectively to the child and the adults responsible for him" (p. 97). This position is valid, we should stress, for all children because all children are vulnerable and the conditions that place their development at risk characterize, to one degree or another, all social and economic groups.

Our position is that the active participation of mental health professionals in the primary care setting is the most promising route to developing the comprehensive programs that are likely to be utilized effectively. In making this recommendation we do not overlook the importance of more effective communication of mental health knowledge in the training of pediatricians, nurses, teachers, and other early childhood specialists. But even given improvement in the breadth of their training there will still be a need for the mental health specialist in the programs important for disadvantaged families.

The indispensable services, in our view, are as follows: (1) health care and health supervision for the child, involving the skills of primary physicians and nurses; (2) services to parents in the form of guidance, counseling, and other supports, involving the skills of clinical social work; (3) child care and education, involving qualified care providers and early childhood educators. The fourth component of the service that was part of our project—developmental evaluation—need not be provided in as much depth as was utilized in our program or as a separate entity. However, following the development of the child and evaluating him through the usual methods of the physician, nurse, or teacher are important in providing guidance to parents and in planning for the child's future.

The basic requirement for achieving excellence of these several services, we believe, is *continuity of competent personnel*. It is important that those who provide the services are adequately qualified to do so. This position should require no defense. Yet it is disturbing how often, particularly in the realm of child care and education, qualifications and competence are disregarded, resulting in grossly inadequate services, especially, though by no means limited to, those developed for the disadvantaged. "Poor services for poor people" is, regrettably, more than a catch phrase.

The issue of continuity of care by a small number of persons has to do with the importance of developing parental confidence in the services they use for their children. Confidence, trust, and effective communication are difficult to develop if parent and child are seen by first one clinician then another. Moreover, the clinician, too, is at a disadvantage in arriving at a diagnosis and giving appropriate advice when child and parent are strangers to him. Lack of confidence in medical advice is known to influence willingness to take medication prescribed for a specific illness, and, even more, it affects the usefulness to parent and child of recommendations about development and behavior.

Much of what is required to make a difference for disadvantaged families depends upon the development of a working relationship that includes (1) on the part of the providers, commitment to and respect for individuality, as well as clinical skills, and (2) on the part of the users, desire for certain services and substantial expectation that the services are at least adequate and the providers trustworthy. It is difficult, more likely impossible, to help young families improve the quality of their lives and enhance the development of their children without these two ingredients. They relate to how parents can learn to help themselves and their children, even when the wider society may be unchanged in its attitudes and biases.

About each of the three types of service recommended—health care, work with parents, and the provision of substitute care and education for young children—we will comment briefly.

HEALTH CARE AND SUPERVISION

Since most parents are aware of needing medical care for their children, pediatric care of the child provides a sound context for providing services. The continuity of health care by one or a small number of professionals (1) creates conditions in which the child's health and development can best be understood and attended to by the practitioners; (2) enhances communication between parents and physician or nurse; (3) promotes parents' use of pediatric care and their confidence in the value of their own observations and judgments; and (4) plays a part in the child's feeling well cared for even though some of what he encounters at the hands of a physician or nurse is painful or frightening.

It is well known that disadvantaged families have far more difficulty in finding such continuity of care than do more advantaged families. And in many instances they have a greater need for competent clinicians who know them and whom they can trust in the care of their young children. For the past forty years at least, the fields of pediatrics and public health have emphasized that health supervision of the child must include attention to psychosocial as well as physical factors (Powers 1949, 1963; Senn 1948; Aldrich 1946; Richmond and Lipton 1961; Senn and Green 1958; Senn and Solnit 1968; M. Lewis 1971; Green and Haggerty 1977). Green (1980), describing the pediatric interview as the basic tool for pediatric diagnosis, emphasizes that it serves both diagnostic and therapeutic goals. He says that the effective pediatric interview is based on a conceptual scheme "that permits a balanced integration of (1) biomedical and biosocial considerations; (2) the child, family and community; and (3) health and disease" (p. 5). He expects, as do we, that most physicians will have been well trained in discussing a presenting complaint and well versed in the content of the systems review and the physical examination. In his plea for expansion of the traditional focus on the chief complaint, Green emphasizes the importance of skillful listening, empathy, warmth and courtesy, and attentive interest. The physician with these qualities and attitudes, he points out, is able to promote confidence and rapport; he has knowledge that gives relief and an understanding of people without a need to moralize, judge, or reprove. He comments that patients want their doctors to care about them. Green, as a leading pediatrician actively involved in caring for children and training others to do so, has articulated principles and recommended practices that describe child health care of excellence for all children. His views are very compatible with our own view of the pediatrician's role in our program.

As to the transferability of health care efforts in respect to disadvantaged families, we can easily envisage a program of excellence in which public health nurses and nurse practitioners provide a major part of the child health care with the physician's support and backup. We can also see an advantage to having family practitioners as primary physicians and extending the service to include medical care for parents as well as children. Whether the primary clinician is a pediatrician, nurse, or family practitioner is less important than that the principles, attitudes, and skills that constitute excellence are at work.

WORKING WITH PARENTS

The work with parents has many facets. To some degree, work with parents is implicit in the notion of providing health care for the child—that is, advice about the child's health and aspects of development and behavior are part of the traditional role of pediatrician, pediatric nurse, and, increasingly, pediatric nurse-practitioner. These practitioners work in a social context, and the relationship between physician or nurse, parents, and child is a vital factor in the effectiveness of health care. However, we hope this report has made it clear that disadvantaged young parents also require assistance in order to develop as parents and to deal with stresses in their lives as adults that are often beyond the purview of the child's practitioner. Such assistance is also beyond the scope of the untrained, friendly "home visitor," although such visitors can provide a certain kind of support not unimportant in itself. Many parents need the specific skills of the clinical social worker. Familiarity with community resources and how to enable the parent to use them is but one aspect of the social worker's role. In addition, the clinical social worker is the professional most often relied upon in child health settings for knowledge in the mental health field.

This is not meant to imply that those working in programs for young families deal mainly with mental illness; in fact they confront a range of problems, from those resulting from day-to-day stresses that depress coping capacity in normal parents, to neurotic problems, to sociopathic and pre- or post-psychotic conditions. A clinical social worker needs the knowledge to differentiate among these kinds of problems and the skill to function effectively with each. In this connection let us emphasize again that the sensitive application of that knowledge is of particular importance. In providing health, education, and social services to the disadvantaged, one needs not only to know what they need or want but to be able to judge whether a service to be offered is both appropriate and timely. How does a clinician's or an educator's view of what might be "good for the child and family" fit with the clients' awareness and readiness? One must distinguish in one's work, for example, between outreach and intrusiveness, between guiding parents and lecturing them, between providing them with the tangible supports they appear to need and enabling them to get these for themselves, between imposing, even in a benevolent fashion, one's own goals for them and helping them to define and consider their goals for themselves. We would add to the general and usual qualifications of the clinical social worker the need for knowledge of early childhood development and the development of parenthood, knowledge generally gained through experience in a setting serving young children and parents. In programs such as ours, and often in other settings, one of the responsibilities of the social worker is to serve as coordinator of the work with children and parents and as liaison with other community resources.

While this role could no doubt be carried out by another, the point is that it is an essential function that must be planned for.

CHILD DAYCARE AND EDUCATION

Substitute child care, particularly daycare that includes educational experiences for young children, is an important service. And it is important, here as elsewhere, that the child care and education be of good quality. For working parents who are disadvantaged, just as for other working parents, daycare is an increasingly important, often essential service. For other disadvantaged parents who choose not to work or who are unemployable for whatever reason, the availability of good child care in an educational setting that welcomes both parents and children provides an opportunity for them to obtain some of the experiences that may be missing from their own daily lives. For parents who are also unable to provide even a reasonably adequate environment responsive to the young child's developmental needs, the daycare setting can serve as an important and rich source of aid. This group includes, for example, parents whose personal problems result in such chaotic, neglectful, markedly inconsistent, or abusive behavior that they require more than ordinary assistance and their children require daily care and often special services from others.

In daycare, as in health care, continuity of care is important both for children and for parents. There is also substantial evidence from a variety of studies that the quality of daycare makes a difference. A number of these studies are presented and evaluated in a recent publication edited by Zigler and Gordon, *Day Care: Scientific and Social Policy Issues* (1982). The concept of developmental daycare, articulated especially since 1970, has largely replaced custodial care as the standard. However, much of the daycare provided both for the disadvantaged and for the more affluent remains inadequate to meet the developmental needs of children and to provide the supports needed by most parents who must leave their young children in the care of others for long hours each day.

Developmental daycare implies the responsibility of adults to provide the children with experiences that facilitate learning, coping behavior, and adaptation. It is of particular importance that those providing care and education for children who are not their own be qualified to do so through their knowledge and personality characteristics. The professional credentials required of those who provide health and social work services are apparent. No less important are the credentials of the educator. It is essential, in our view, that those who are in leadership positions be qualified through training in early childhood education and child development and that they have the ability to supervise the work of others and to facilitate the learning of those with less training. Similarly, since the partnership with parents in behalf of the child and the supportive communication with and guidance of parents are so important, it is essential that the providers of such services pay close attention to the qualifications and size of the staff. Even a very competent staff cannot be effective if the staff-child ratio is unfavorable and if staff members are not available when parents need to talk with them. At its best, daycare combines individualized, affectionate nurturance, approximating the kind given by a good parent, with the sensitivity, perceptiveness, teaching skills, and child development knowledge of the competent early childhood educator.

An essential condition in our view is that child-care and education services be closely coordinated with health and social work services. It is less important that they be under the same roof—although so doing facilitates coordination—than that the three services function in harmony.

To recapitulate, we see the following as essential components of an effective program for assisting disadvantaged young parents and their children:

1. Making a clear statement of concepts from theory and/or practice that guide the program's daily work and planning
2. Including in the primary care system knowledge derived from theory and practice in psychiatry, clinical social work, and psychology
3. Assuring competence and continuity of services and of the personnel providing them

4. Extending health care to the child that includes attention to development by primary clinicians—namely, pediatrician, nurse, family practitioner, and their allies
5. Offering services to parents which involve the skills of clinical social work, including knowledge of child development and parenthood
6. Providing child daycare and education including attention to the child's progress provided by qualified child caregivers and early childhood educators
7. Coordinating closely the efforts of physician, social worker, and teacher
8. Caring about those one serves

The omission of any of these components, we believe, will render the services less effective than they can be. It should be obvious that those providing the services must be qualified to do so. Nevertheless, the best work requires both a continuing dialogue about the most significant methods of practice and the close coordination of efforts in the three central service areas. The last essential, caring about those one serves, may seem too obvious to warrant inclusion. However, the human, empathic concern of one person for another is so important and influential that it deserves emphasis.

Even if all the kinds of services recommended are provided, and provided effectively, we do not assume that this will solve more than a few of the problems faced by the disadvantaged members of our society. Please recall that in the case examples given earlier the records reveal differences in the manner and extent of the benefit which families received through participation in the program. This should not be surprising since despite their similarities there were large variations among the parents with respect to endowment, general adaptive abilities, personality characteristics, and capacity for relating, trusting others, and developing as parents. They varied widely in their childhood experiences, including the strengths in their families of origin and the quality of their nurturance, conditions that influenced their functioning as adults.

This study does, however, suggest—and so we believe—that once good services are made available by qualified personnel who respect those they serve and who appreciate how complex human behavior is, the services can make a difference in their lives. What will be utilized depends also upon the participants, since what they bring to the situation has a bearing on what each can use from it. And further, if a spectrum of quality services is provided that offers options responsive to the needs of individual participants, the evidence of this study is that these services will influence favorably the lives of a large majority of participants. The influence appears to be both immediate and long lasting.

APPENDIXES

Some Observations and Comments on Daycare

Learning from Ordinary Experiences

Miss T. held Terry, 4 months, on her lap, putting an interesting toy in front of him. She talked about the toy and through the social contact stimulated his use of it, helping him to handle first one toy and then another. Later she placed him in an infant seat in his crib, close enough to the mobile attached to the crib that he could touch and grasp the bright sponge-rubber animals.

While the caregiver might do much the same thing with any young infant, there was a particular reason for working with Terry as Miss T. did. He was a tense, jittery baby, and his tension was heightened because his normal motor abilities were lagging behind his advanced visual discrimination. Helping him to be more active with the toys helped to relieve a part of his muscular tension but also promoted his learning.

Leslie, 4 months, being bathed by Miss T., was relaxed and smiling as Miss T. talked with her and put a small red plastic fish into the water to attract her. She watched it intently, flailed her arms, splashing the water and trying to get the fish. The splashing fascinated her and she continued it, delighted by the new experience. Miss T. talked to her about what was happening. Later Leslie was equally interested in watching Miss T. squeeze water out of a sponge. Then she noticed the fish again and after several attempts managed to grasp it with both hands, a new accomplishment for her.

The learning potential for Leslie in this situation is evident both in what Miss T. did and did not do. Throughout the bath she talked to Leslie, rather than silently and in a businesslike way making the

sole object of bathing the achievement of cleanliness. She didn't try
to stop Leslie's splashing but enjoyed it with her. The bathing process was not only an enjoyable social experience for Leslie but one
in which she discovered her ability to splash and succeeded for the
first time in grasping a floating object.

From the toys and supplies available, Terry, 10 months, selected
a margarine cup and a popsicle stick. On the floor he hit the cup
several times with the stick, causing it to flip over. Then, using the
stick again, he scooted the cup along the floor. He continued for ten
minutes with great concentration, alternately flipping and pushing
the cup and observing what happened. Later when he was in the
kitchen with Miss T., he came upon the open dishwasher. He found
he could roll the lower rack in and out. He continued, smiling with
pleasure as he listened to the changing clatter of the dishes. Then he
poked around in the soap well for several minutes. All of this was
done in an exploratory manner. Miss T. commented occasionally about
what he was doing but allowed him to carry through his "project"
in his own way.

This observation indicates the concentration of which a 10-month-
old infant is capable, demonstrates that many an educational toy is
in no catalogue and that, if adults are perceptive and supportive, a
child can learn from almost anything in his environment. It would
have been an unwarranted interruption of self-initiated exploration
if someone had insisted on substituting a "proper" toy. At other times
during the day Terry, of course, was involved in adult-initiated learning
experiences.

Based on endowment, Shawn, 17 months, was delayed in speech
and other aspects of his cognitive development. For a time he was
interested in only two things, large muscle activity and food. We
could use the former only a little to stimulate his speech, but his love
of eating could be put to good use. It was possible to interest him in
the names of food, the implements he was using, and the qualities of
food. Around this situation he could listen and respond much better
than in any other. The situation also facilitated the development of
eye-hand coordination as he became interested in helping to feed
himself. We used mealtime as a learning opportunity as well as a

social experience for all children, but with Shawn for a time it was especially important as our most effective means of encouraging learning.

There are, of course, countless opportunities for learning in day-care. The examples we have cited are only a few of the less obvious.

Interpreting Infant Behavior

Sitting on the floor with Terry, 8 months, Leslie, also 8 months, watched him play with an hourglass containing colorful beads. She looked intently as he turned it in his hands, then reached over and took it from him. Terry didn't protest but Miss T. handed him an-other one. Leslie then dropped hers and took his, repeating this three more times, always wanting the toy Terry had. At last Terry protested, crying. Miss T. then stepped in, separated the babies, and gave one of the toys to each.

It is not likely that at 8 months Leslie learned anything about the rights of others. What is more important is that Miss T.'s behavior was appropriate to the situation: She did not assume Leslie's behav-ior at 8 months meant she selfishly wanted all the toys for herself. Instead Miss T. thought Leslie was attracted by the toy when it was animated by Terry's handling of it, not realizing that she could create the same visual effect with her own. Thus Miss T., fascinated by what was going on, replaced Terry's lost toy each time and inter-vened only when Terry clearly needed more help.

In only two months' time, at 10 months, there was a shift in the meaning of Leslie's behavior with David, a month younger. He had a cup she wanted. He didn't let go when she pulled at it. She then grabbed at his nose and his shirt, pulling him toward her with loud scolding noises. Later she tried to take his ball, but again he held on. She scolded him but didn't touch him. Still later she succeeded in getting some tricolored rings away from him. Though David did nothing but look at her, she shook them vigorously in front of him and yelled crossly at him as if warning him not to try anything.

Now Leslie seemed to react to David as a threat to what she wanted. The confrontation between the two infants is an example of many

that take place every day when young children are together. Involved are interpersonal negotiations, important aspects of learning,
in which adults are often required to act as mediators. Many such
episodes if accompanied by appropriate adult intervention can begin
to create awareness of the needs and wishes of others.

Meeting Individual Needs at Mealtime

Put in his high chair for lunch, Jackie, 12 months, was quiet while
Miss T. put Joan, 15 months, in a high chair and sat down between
them. Joan was very hungry and irritable so Miss T. served her first.
Jackie began to fuss when he saw her food. Miss T. then put small
pieces of meat and a few string beans on his high-chair tray, and
Jackie quieted for about five minutes as he picked up and ate his
food. He listened as Miss T. talked to Joan about what she was
eating and how well she used her spoon. Later when Jackie was fed
pudding he insisted on holding the spoon, so Miss T. took another.
Joan was now smearing food on her tray, but Miss T. did not interfere. With help from Miss T., Jackie held a small glass of milk and
drank from it, spilling part. Then he slid down in his chair, rubbed
his eyes, looked sleepy and tired. Miss T. lifted him out of the high
chair and held him on her lap as she helped Joan finish lunch. Joan
played on the floor as Miss T. washed Jackie's hands and face and
prepared him for his nap.

This peaceful lunch period could have been a disaster without the
skill of the caregiver and her knowledge of what each child was
ready for. Miss T. knew that Jackie was able to pick up small bits of
food and get them to his mouth, and she made it possible for him to
do so. Joan, 3 months older, could do more self-feeding. Miss T. was
also able to respond sensitively to the cues from each child as to their
feelings and needs. Each child was allowed as much initiative and as
much help as needed; Miss T. avoided the tendency of some adults
either to do all the feeding or to expect the child to do it alone.
Acceptance of some messiness is necessary as well as patience and
enjoyment of only gradual improvement in self-feeding skills.

Toddlers Attempt to Persuade

David, 17 months, wanted to get into a large cardboard box with Terry, 18 months. When Terry wouldn't let him, David went looking for a toy, and came back dragging one on the floor just enough out of Terry's reach so he couldn't grab it. As it would get very close to Terry, David, grinning mischievously, would pull it farther away.

Both teasing and problem-solving strategy were involved in David's behavior. One wonders whether he had copied the diversionary tactics he had observed the staff use in substituting one plaything for another. Below examples are given of older children's attempts to use verbal persuasion to get the playthings they wanted.

Larry, 27 months, did his best to talk Paul, 25 months, out of the steering wheel toy so he could have it. He said excitedly, "Paul, go ride the scooter—see the scooter," pointing to it. Paul held fast to the steering wheel, and after Larry's repeated attempts at persuasion failed, he settled for finding a tricycle.

Larry's attempt at persuasion was much more sophisticated than that of David at 17 months. Larry's method represents a technique that was used by several of the children by the time they were age 2 and over. However, the same children who were capable of using words and gestures at one time might at another time resort to grabbing what they wanted or hitting the child who had it. Still another strategy was used in the following example.

Jackie, 26 months, got off his kiddy car and decided he wanted his favorite trike, which Paul, 29 months had. Jackie got a shovel, took it to Paul, and talked to him, trying to get him to trade. Paul wouldn't relinquish it in spite of Jackie's efforts.

Calm to Chaos: Implications for Staff-Child Ratio

Greg, David, Terry and Leslie, all 16 to 17 months, and Shawn, 14 months, were playing peacefully when Miss T. left the nursery to get something from the kitchen. Almost at once she heard shrill screaming. She returned to find all the children shrieking at one another and aggressively taking things away from each other. The atmosphere was one of tension and contagious excitement. Miss T. was told by the other teacher present that when Greg started to push the small cart, Shawn wanted it also, and a tug-of-war ensued. The teacher had interceded but not quickly enough to succeed in diverting Shawn's attention to another plaything. The struggle between Greg and Shawn had set off the other children, and by the time Greg gained undisputed possession of the cart, he was too upset to enjoy it, and collapsed on the floor in frustrated crying.

This incident illustrates how a situation involving young toddlers can go from calm to chaos in a matter of seconds. While it is appropriate to let children try to work things out up to a point, at this age they can seldom reach an equitable solution. If occurrences like this are frequent, they interfere with the children's ability to play and to learn. Probably no one adult left with five toddlers could mediate all the struggles that might arise in the course of a few minutes—one of the reasons why staff-child ratios satisfactory for older children are inadequate for toddlers. The next example is of a circumstance involving two older children in which they were appropriately allowed to try to work out of a fight.

Greg and Terry, both 23 months, were with Miss T. in the staff lounge. No other children were present. Greg was sitting on the floor looking at a book. When Terry approached and tried to grab the book, a fight ensued in which Greg hit out at Terry several times. Terry had a grip on Greg's shirt and persisted in trying to get the book. They were evenly matched and neither was able to victimize the other, so Miss T. allowed the contest to go on for about a minute. Terry finally managed to pull Greg to the floor. Then Miss T. good-naturedly separated them. The book was restored to Greg and Terry was given another. In a few minutes the two boys were in a friendly mood, sitting close together sharing a cushion, each looking at his book.

It is always a matter of judgment in each situation as to when to intervene. Had the fight occurred in one of the playrooms with other children who were becoming upset by it, the teacher might have decided to intervene sooner, especially if there were not enough adults present to deal with the reactions of all the children.

Naptime, a Time of Vulnerability

Greg, 18 months, was quite upset when he was put down for a nap on a cot his first day in the program after being away a month. He cried and got up, finding no comfort in his usually beloved bottle as an aid in going to sleep. Miss T., who was nearby, rocked him and sang to him, but when put back on his cot he began to fuss again. Miss T. then sat by him, rubbed his back, and talked softly to him, and he was soon asleep.

This was not only Greg's first day back after a month's absence; it was his first experience of being on a cot instead of in a crib, probably a mistake in timing. However, with the availability of a familiar adult to acknowledge his distress and take appropriate action, he was easily comforted. Ignoring distress in such situations or punishing would not only increase distress but prolong it.

Imitation and Identification

Steven, 23 months, and Jackie, 21 months, observed Sybil, 21 months, arriving for her first day in toddler school, hesitate shyly at the door. Each picked up a toy and went to her, offering it and extending his hand to try to get her to come into the room.

The first incident of one child attempting to help another occurred when the two children involved were 15 months. Such behavior was not often seen until 17 to 18 months. Thereafter many incidents occurred which we understood at first simply as imitation of adult behavior, but as affective elements began to appear along with the helpful action, we felt identification with staff and/or parent behavior was involved. Examples were given in Chapter 4, page 82, and others are given below. We believe these are important indicators of the children's perceptions of how *they* were nurtured in daycare. One of the children very helpful to others was Jackie, who at home was poorly cared for, even abused, as we described in *The Challenge of Daycare*. Yet he could differentiate between the two settings and his care in each.

David, 19 months, came over and handed Leslie, 20 months, a butter tin, something she had always taken on entering the room but had not been able to find this morning. As David handed it to her, he said, "Here," and Leslie took it, saying, "Thank you." Both smiled slightly at one another.

Jackie, 23 months, was at the blackboard using chalk, having been given a piece of Kleenex to use as an eraser. When another child joined him, Jackie asked the teacher to "get 'raser for him too."

Steven, 25 months, cared for a baby doll quite tenderly, carrying it cradled in his arm, gently rocking it. He got a bottle and fed the doll while he sat holding it. Then he took the doll for a ride in the rocking boat. In all he carried it around with him for ten minutes, seeming to be very conscious of the doll's comfort the whole time. Steven had need-satisfying care at Children's House but also, especially during the first 15 months of life, at home from his mother.

When Steven, 27 months, was lying on the floor, Larry, 29 months, got down beside him and noticed that he needed a tissue. He held Steven's hands so that he couldn't use them and said to a staff member, "He need a tissue. Get a tissue."

Larry's behavior was probably not perceived by Steven as helpful. In this instance, Larry may have seen himself as assisting the staff. The hand-holding technique was one his mother used with him. In the next observation also, Larry acts more out of his own need than the need of the other child.

At lunch Larry, 29 months, noticed that Paul, 27 months, had cake icing on his fingers. Larry said, "Give me that rag." He carefully cleaned off Paul's hand while Paul went on eating. Larry had a purposeful air about him as he attended to Paul. Paul wasn't the least concerned about the icing, but he tolerated Larry's concerned ministrations.

Larry's behavior probably reflected his own concern about getting dirty (he was being toilet trained) as well as an imitation of his mother's behavior with him. In this instance he was also copying staff behavior, but his timing was wrong. A staff member would have allowed Paul to enjoy his cake and only then cleaned his fingers.

David, 27 months, was helping Jackie, 14 months, get into a cabinet used for separation and reunion games. Jackie was holding the door in such a way that his fingers might get pinched. David noticed and said, "Watch your fingers, Jackie." Then he opened the door and moved Jackie's fingers out of the way.

Involved were not only help to another child and identification with adults, but David's ability to anticipate the cause-and-effect relationship in this situation, to warn with words, but when words brought no response, to take appropriate action.

Toilet Training

Miss T. took Curtis, 24 months, to the child-size toilet three times in the course of the morning. He went along agreeably, sat willingly, looked relaxed, and didn't get up until invited, but neither did he urinate. Shortly after being diapered, he wet but showed no awareness that he had.

Curtis was both unaware of body sensations at this time and undisturbed by being wet. However, his grandmother wanted to start his training, so we began also. The observation above is of typical behavior around our efforts at this time. Had it not been for our wish to cooperate with Curtis's grandmother, we would not have started training, since he was giving none of the signals of readiness. In contrast, Steven's training was begun both at home and in the center as the result of mutual agreement about his readiness when he was 20 months. Out in the yard one day when he was 22 months he said something in turn to three different staff members. No one could understand what he said. Soon he had a bowel movement in his pants and announced it by saying, "Poopee." His regular caregiver, not present because of illness, would have understood his first communication. Thereafter all staff understood and responded promptly to his signal. He was singularly unresistant and cooperative not only in toilet training but in situations of eating, sleeping, being dressed or undressed, a commentary on his mother's ability to deal with him without letting any issue become an intense problem.

Leslie's training began when she was 19 months and was accomplished by 26 months. She put up little resistance when her principal caregiver could be with her; a little more, if not. Shortly after her achievement she showed her knowledge of the process one morning and her identification with the staff by helping David, 25 months, with his toileting. When he clutched his penis, she took him by the hand, led him to the bathroom, helped him pull his pants down and get on the toilet seat. After he urinated, he got off the toilet, smiling. Leslie clapped and cheered. Then she helped him pull up his pants, he flushed the toilet, and they went back to the playroom obviously pleased with themselves.

Taking Turns

David, 26 months, and Shawn and Peter, both 23 months, were all interested in the xylophone Miss T. showed them. She sat on the rug with it, and the children joined her there. She said that Peter would have a turn first, then Shawn, and then David. She kept the turns brief and assured them they would each have a turn. They were free to leave, but all three remained interested and involved, each enjoying the sound he and the others made. Both serious attention and exuberant pleasure were apparent.

In such a situation keeping the one and only instrument under close control was important; so was keeping the turns brief and giving reassurance. Of course, having a pleasant shared experience was also possible because the children knew Miss T. well and trusted her. The next two examples show more active acceptance of sharing, but also some reluctance about it.

Jackie, 24 months, and Paul, 27 months, were in the backyard playing with a ball. Miss T. encouraged them to take turns throwing it at the cellar door and getting it as it rolled down the door. Jackie kept the play going by saying each time, "Jackie's turn," and "Your turn," to Paul. After a while the game was about to break up with

Paul holding on to the ball. Jackie went to the other end of the yard to get a ball and brought it, saying to Paul, "More ball, more ball."

Paul, 30 months, was greatly enjoying sitting on top of the toy gas pump in the yard surveying the landscape. After he had been there a while, he heard Miss T. say something to Steven, who was waiting for a turn. Paul said, "Steven's turn?" and when asked if that was all right, said, "OK." Almost immediately after Steven was put up on the pump, Paul said, "My turn, my turn." He was, however, able to wait a reasonable length of time.

In the earlier example of children waiting for turns with the xylophone, the teacher necessarily kept close control of the situation. By now while there was variation in the children's ability to wait turns, they all appeared to understand the concept of turns and to wait their turn much of the time.

Make-believe

Leslie at 15 months was observed holding out her hands to David, 14 months, as if offering him something. When he reached for it, she quickly drew her hands back and put them to her mouth. She went through chewing motions, smacked her lips, and smiled.

Teasing was obviously involved in Leslie's behavior, but of interest in the present context is her ability to engage in a bit of make-believe play. Elementary forms of imaginary play were seen as early as 15 months, with several of the children imitating the miming behavior of staff, stirring in empty cups and bowls, and going through the motions of feeding themselves and others. From that point on teachers consistently used various opportunities to help the children expand the themes of play and increase their ability to sustain it. Subjects around which suggestions were made for make-believe play were those within the children's experience. The repertoire was enlarged as they grew older and their experiences and interests widened, partly as a result of what they were offered in daycare. The earliest examples were of self-feeding and feeding a child or adult. Next came feeding of dolls and gradually more elaborated forms of baby care, putting to bed, diapering, bathing. Other themes that

developed with teacher help were the following, though not necessarily in the order given: having telephone conversations; driving
cars and trucks, putting gas in them and repairing them; dressing
up to go someplace, using real props such as hats, pocketbooks,
scarves; cooking and serving food, again with pots and pans, a toy
stove, and dishes as props but with the food imagined; going to the
store, buying something, and returning with it; going on a bus trip
by means of lined up chairs; playing at being a doctor or a patient.
Usually even up to age 30 months teacher's questions or suggestions
were necessary to get the first make-believe play of any kind started,
and the teacher's presence was necessary to keep it going.

Paul, 27 months, took the toy cash register to a table. After
watching him play with it for a few minutes, Eric, 27 months, wanted
it. He was given another one, and the two sat together, each exper-
imenting with his toy's possibilities. Jackie, 24 months, Steven, 27
months, and Larry, 29 months, came over and watched. Miss T. said
they could all play store; some could buy and some could sell. She
further set up the play by pretending to have money and wanting to
buy some food. Soon all the children were busy buying and selling.
When Miss T. finished her purchases, she went "home" to the
housekeeping corner, laid out an imaginary meal, returned to the
store, and asked if anyone would like to come to her house for din-
ner. Paul, Larry, and Jackie came, and after eating and appearing to
enjoy their meal, they fed their babies and put them to bed. Later
when Paul and Larry were holding their babies, Steven lay down
on the floor, pretending to cry like a baby. Miss T. suggested that
the baby needed something; maybe he was hungry. Steven nodded
his head vigorously in assent. Paul and Larry fed him until he no
longer cried, but they decided to check him over with the stethoscope. Satisfied, they returned to their babies.

The sequence above illustrates the important role of the teacher
in making it possible for children this age to carry on more than
fragmentary imaginative play.

For reasons that we did not always understand, some children,
advanced in other ways, were slow to move into pretending. One
child at 24 months with advanced language and social skills was still

having trouble with the concept of pretending and was sometimes puzzled and upset by make-believe play in others. The most he could manage at that age was to pretend he was having a telephone conversation. However, by 27 months he could do a little more; for example, approaching Miss T. one day with the toy stethoscope, he listened to her heart, saying, "You're all right," and walked away adding, "I'm a baby doctor." In contrast, another child, who was much less skillful verbally and whose play was dominated in the second year by manipulative toys and large muscle activity, at 27 months suddenly began using a dollhouse and doll figures to carry out domestic play. His play seems to have enabled another child to move into similar play and extend it as illustrated below.

Curtis, 27 months, spent much of the morning playing with the doll furniture and people. The last time the staff had provided the children with similar play materials only a month before no one was able to use them, but now the play was quite well developed. Curtis arranged the furniture in the house in the various rooms and assigned roles to the dolls. Larry, 29 months, was an observer of Curtis's play. The next day Larry repeated the play and elaborated it a bit, putting the dolls in chairs, then having them go for a ride and come back and go to bed. Two days later Curtis engaged Miss T. in some prolonged pretend play that included going for a ride in the car, stopping at McDonald's to get food for everyone, and then visiting friends.

In the next examples the play is initiated and carried on for a few minutes by two children without adult participation, but eventually intercession is necessary.

Paul, 27 months, and Jackie, 24 months, are in rocking chairs at the housekeeping corner table. They rock and sip "coffee." Jackie is restless and shortly gets up and runs off, but Paul continues to rock quietly. Then he gets up, goes to the stove, takes something out of a big pot on the stove with a spoon, fills his bowl, puts the spoon back in the pot. He starts to sit down but Jackie returns, so he serves him in the same fashion and begins to add a second helping. Jackie picks up his bowl shouting, "No more!" Paul scowls and serves himself again. Jackie grabs the serving spoon from Paul shouting, "Mine!"

With trouble about to erupt, Miss T. intervenes, gives the spoon back to Paul and takes Jackie off to find another. Paul sits down again, eats his food, and says, "Mm, mm." Finding himself alone, he takes his bowl over to a teacher who is nearby and offers her some. Then he wanders in the direction of the chalk board.

In our program we emphasized development of the capacity to use make-believe because of its importance in problem solving, in mastering new experiences, and in fostering various kinds of creativity and symbolic thinking. Children who for various reasons do not have access to imaginative play are deprived of a useful way of coping with stress.

Partners in Play

Jackie, 23 months, and Curtis, 29 months, each picked up a large cardboard box and beat on it as they paraded around the room. Steven, 26 months, watched for a minute, then joined in. The three marched around and around the table beating in unison and getting louder and louder. Then Steven asked for music to be turned on and they continued both marching and dancing to the music for about 15 minutes.

Earlier in the year teachers had sponsored similar activities and thereafter children spontaneously began them.

Larry, 27 months, rode the horse most of the time for thirty minutes, obviously playing cowboy. But he wanted someone to join him and kept calling to various other children, "Hey, come ride the horsie." Finally Paul, 25 months, joined him.

Having a partner in play by now had become quite important to most of the children. In fact, as the next example illustrates, feelings about the child who deserted a shared activity could be strong and result in seemingly unprovoked aggression.

Paul, 29 months, and Jackie, 26 months, were going back and forth from the sink, where they were allowed a few drops of water in cups, to the housekeeping corner, taking turns repeatedly. There had been no squabbling between the two. But Paul, tiring of the activity, walked away. Jackie stopped what he was doing at the sink and stared after Paul. Then he darted toward him, pushed him squarely in the back causing him to fall flat on his face. Paul cried angrily, and Jackie ran away looking pleased with himself.

Playfulness

Steven, 28 months, spent fifty minutes on Miss T.'s lap looking at books. Despite many distractions, he always returned his attention to exchanges with her about the pictures. Once after he had correctly named many objects, Miss T. playfully called all of the different bugs on a page grasshoppers. Steven was delighted. He continued naming objects in still another book, and then called a bumblebee a kitty cat, laughing gleefully.

Steven had been fully aware of the playfulness of Miss T. calling the bugs all grasshoppers, and he enjoyed the opportunity to show her that he, too, could play that way. Attempts to encourage playfulness must, of course, be made only when one knows a child well enough to be sure playfulness, not confusion, will result.

Toddlers in Conflict

Curtis, 18 months, was playing with a car. When Leslie, 26 months, took it away, he burst into tears and stood still, seeming to be immobilized.

Leslie, 19 months, who often exhibited unprovoked aggression and indiscriminate snatching of other's toys, had recently been reacting with fear when no threat from another child was involved. Today when Greg, 19 months, arrived and joined in the play, Leslie became very watchful. Any time he came toward her holding an object in his hand or even dragging one behind him, she would cry out and run to a teacher for protection. Then when Shawn, 16 months, came she showed the same behavior toward him.

When Joan, 18 months, took the workbench away from Larry, 19 months, he looked upset and protested vocally but did not try to get it back. Miss T. suggested he could have tried harder to hang on to it. Later when Paul, 18 months, tried to take it from him, he succeeded in keeping it.

Jackie, 18 months, and Larry, 22 months, were riding kiddy cars.

When they rode into the next room, Larry greeted Paul, 20 months, saying, "Hi." Paul grabbed Larry's kiddy car and held on. Larry shouted, "No! Me! Me! Me!" But Paul held on and hit Larry, who started to cry. Miss T. intervened with Paul, but even so Larry threw himself on the floor sobbing angrily.

Jackie, 26 months, and Steven, 28 months, both ran toward a kiddy car and arrived at the same time. They struggled for a few seconds, each grabbing. Then Steven got on it. Jackie ran over to Miss T. saying, "Give me a kiddy car," and led her to the garage to get another one.

Jackie showed Miss T. a scratch on his arm and said accusingly, "Stee! Stee!" Miss T. said, "You'll have to tell Steven not to do that." Jackie frowned, got up and went over to Steven, hit him on the head and said angrily, "No!" and walked away.

Juvenile Justice

Leslie and Terry, both 20 months, and Curtis, 12 months, were in the room together. Terry went over to Curtis and took a toy away from him. Leslie then went to Terry and said, "No, his," took the toy from Terry, and gave it back to Curtis.

Ideas of ownership can be recognized early when the child's own wish to possess is not involved. Leslie had been unusually concerned with what she considered the misdeeds of other children, probably in response to pressure put on her at home. Over a period of several months she had frequently had to be told that another child's behavior was not her concern, that the teachers would worry about it. When she was 28 months, one day she started to scold at Terry, also 28 months, but stopped herself and said, "Not my worry."

Sharing

Paul, 27 months, came in with a small box of wafers. He carefully doled them out to Jackie, Steven, Curtis, and himself. He seemed to take it for granted that they were for everyone.

Curtis, 30 months, arrived eating an apple. He made the rounds giving Jackie and Steven a bite. He also offered a bite to Miss T.

Darlene, 20 months, was sitting with Miss T. stringing beads. Curtis, 18 months, watched solemnly from a distance and then came over smiling. He leaned against Miss T. and reached toward Darlene's beads. When Darlene pulled back, Miss T. said, "I guess Darlene doesn't want to share her beads." Darlene then smiled, said, "Here," and handed Curtis a bead. Curtis went to get himself a chair, and all three sat together working with the beads.

Affectionate Behavior and "Friendships"

Curtis, 17 months, and David, 25 months, were sitting together being quite friendly. Curtis put his arm around David and looked at him, smiling.

Curtis, 24 months, spent a lot of time this morning close to Steven, 21 months. Curtis acted as if he were trying to protect or take care of Steven, holding his hand and putting his arm around him. Later when we went for a walk, Curtis wanted to hold Steven's hand.

Leslie, 27 months, on Miss T.'s lap, reached for Curtis, 19 months, and patting him on the head, tried to kiss him.

As Larry, 30 months, was leaving, Jackie, 25 months, said, "See you tomorrow," and patted him on the shoulder.

Several times today Steven, 29 months, hugged and kissed Jackie, 26 months, on the cheek after he had refused to play with him as Jackie requested.

The above examples of affectionate behavior are typical of many that occurred, none of which was prompted by adult suggestion. Steven's behavior with Jackie exemplifies also the special ties which developed between several pairs of children. The first of these "friendships" began between David and Leslie when they were 17 and 18 months. It was somewhat more the result of activity on David's part than Leslie's in that he tried to help her, to look after her interests, and to comfort her. But Leslie preferred him to the other children and appeared to enjoy his attention. The illustration of helping behavior given earlier—David's finding the butter tin for

Leslie—is illustrative also of the beginning of their special tie. Other examples follow.

David, 24 months, burst into the room and ran to the rocking boat where Leslie, 25 months, was sitting. She smiled and said, "Hi, David, David, hi." He got into the boat and sat across from her. A big smile on her face, Leslie leaned forward putting her hands on either side of David's face and gave him a kiss.

Two other children who developed an especially strong bond were Steven and Jackie. Two examples were given in Chapter 4, page 82, of Steven comforting Jackie. Their pleasure in one another's company is illustrated in the examples below.

Told that Steven, 27 months, was arriving, Jackie, 24 months, ran to the back door saying, "Stee, Stee." Miss T. opened the door for Jackie and he sailed out, down the steps, and across the yard to Steven at the gate. Jackie peered into Steven's face as he took his hand and walked with him back to the house. They talked together as though they were buddies who hadn't seen each other for ages.

There was a party for Jackie, 26 months, who was leaving daycare, temporarily as it turned out. Steven, 29 months, sat next to Jackie. They talked together and dipped their spoons gleefully into each other's ice cream. Jackie put his finger on Steven's cheek, at which Steven rolled his eyes and made a joyful sound. Jackie again touched Steven's cheek, and Steven turned and kissed his hand. Then Jackie gave Steven some of his cake icing, saying, "Here, you eat it."

When Jackie visited Children's House three months after it closed, he was playing with some of the familiar daycare toys. He put several aside, saying they were for "Stee." There had been no prior mention of Steven by the staff member who saw Jackie. His special feeling for Steven had been retained.

Outline for Recording
Social Work Data

Interval Family Narrative, from all sources of information and brief "scenario" of visit.

1. The family unit; identifying information
    Immediate family:
    The following information is to be supplied for each person living in the household, with notation of changes when made: name, age, sex, race, religion, marital status, date of marriage(s), date of separation(s) or divorce(s) if any, family role, education, occupation, earnings
    Extended family:
    The same information as above when relevant; comments about the amount of contact and quality of relationship between immediate and extended families
2. Ethnic background of parents, cultural background, nature of influences on family life
3. Socioeconomic status of parents
    Information concerning general socioeconomic background and current status, attitudes toward and aspirations to change.
4. The physical environment
    Description of the neighborhood
    Description of the house or apartment exterior, including general appearance, outdoor play space, safety for young children, play equipment
    Description of the house or apartment interior, including general appearance, cleanliness, order, attractiveness, condition of furnishings

187

Number of rooms, relevant aspects of floor plan and space, for example, eating and sleeping arrangements, bathroom, adequacy of space for family life

Play space

Variety and condition of toys and play equipment

Books and other materials appropriate for intellectual stimulation of young children

Evidences of parental interests, hobbies, study.

5. Physical characteristics of parents and changes as they occur
6. Health of parents as reported by parents and observed
7. Information about parental background
8. Impressions of parental personality characteristics with supporting data if possible; interviewer's impression of each parent's self-image, with emphasis on changes
9. Impressions of the marital relationship with supporting data if possible
10. Impression of affective atmosphere of the environment
11. Health of child as reported by parent and as observed in home visit
12. Observations of child-care practices and interaction between parent and child. Describe episodes as they involve the following when they occur during a home visit:

Physical Needs

Feeding

Sleeping

Bathing

Dressing, Undressing, Changing

Play with Toys

Social Interaction

Moments of Peace

Use the following for ways of thinking about the episodes. Comments which are especially interpretive should be included in a separate paragraph:

Type and Quality of Contact:

Modality involved (touch, vision, speech, physical handling, other)

Intensity of contact or child's response

Affect of parents (friendly, unfriendly, angry, other)

Awareness of child's feelings and parents' response (including ability to adapt to child)

Response to child's distress or pleasure

Over- and under-stimulation

Parents' investment of activity (e.g., play with toys or motor activity)

Parental feelings about child at time of any episode

Amount of choice left to child (e.g., termination of feeding, freedom of movement, freedom to explore) and setting of limits and prohibitions (including protection from hazards)

What parent does that promotes or impedes child's development

13. Interviewer's overall assessment of parental feelings toward study-child. Include information about the pregnancy, antepartum expectations about the child in relation to reality, the experience of labor, first reactions to the infant. Include feelings about sex of child, physical appearance, preferred modes of tension discharge, tempo, developmental pace, emerging personality traits

14. Consistency of care: number of caregivers, routine, predictability of parent's behavior

15. Parental report of study-child's development since last interview

16. Parental report of problems in regard to study-child, including problems of feelings toward child

17. Parental report of other problems in family including feelings about members of family, about study procedures or study personnel

18. Other relevant information or impressions not included elsewhere

19. Interviewer's impressions of parental reactions to the interview situation, ease or stress in discussing problem areas, significant omissions in spontaneous productions. Supportive and interventive aspects of the home visitor's contact: interviewer's de-

scription of advice sought and/or given; description of other supportive or interventive measures; assessment of parental ability to seek and use (a) child-care advice, (b) suggestions for alleviating reality problems, (c) psychological help

20. Interviewer's assessment of child's progress and/or problems from home-visit observation. Include assessment of child's use of toys and ability to play with parent, by himself, with peers when age-appropriate. Include also assessment of child's ability to relate to parents, siblings, others in environment

21. "Alerting" statements for subsequent contact of social worker and other staff, questions raised by this contact, "danger signals," unexpected strengths or adaptations, etc.

Outline for Recording Summary of Pediatrician's Regular Health Examination

The pediatrician will write, *after each regular health examination*, a summary to include the following content areas. Begin with relevant interval data and conditions of examination.

1. Growth
2. Illnesses and accidents (circumstances, reactions, outcome)
3. Feeding and oral behavior
4. Elimination and toilet training
5. Sleep
6. Activity and motor development (including impressions of energy and drive)
7. Expressiveness
   a. Vocalizations and speech
   b. Emotion (pleasure-displeasure, crying, etc.)
8. Responses to people (parent, pediatrician, others)
9. Reactions to and use of inanimate object
10. Reactions to own body and self
11. Sensory-perceptive
    a. Skin
    b. Auditory
    c. Visual
    d. Proprioceptive
12. Physical care (impressions of adequacy of)
13. Family and home (as reported by parents)
14. Predominant impressions of parents and some estimate of how this influences the child
15. Physical examination (including neurological)

16. Advice—recommendations—immunizations—treatment
17. Alerting statements (including predictions) for future contact

After any other medically oriented contact of the pediatrician with or about the child there will be a note made on the health record of the reason for the contact, findings, observations, and recommendations. These notations will be included in the summary of the next visit as *Interval Data* wherever relevant.

Observation Categories
for Infants in Daycare

The following is the outline for scheduled observations in selected areas. Not all categories should necessarily be done on the same day, but there should be an observation in each category once every two weeks.

Date: Name of child:

Setting of observation (with description of nursery and persons present)

Situational observations

    Arrival

    Departure and return of mother or her surrogate

    Feeding

    Bath

    Diapering and dressing

    Sleeping

    Preferred activities and materials

    Reaction to strangers

    Reaction to physical discomfort

Developmental observations

    Activity and motor development

    Interaction with people (mother, staff, others, including other babies)

    Language

    Emotional expressiveness and mood

    Play and the use of toys

    Self-stimulating activities

Observer:

Reports of Two
Developmental Examinations

Joan O. Age: 51 weeks

After observing Joan in the daycare program for a few minutes, her mother brought her upstairs for her development test. I began the test with Joan in the high chair and her mother seated nearby but soon had to shift her to her mother's lap because she kept wanting and apparently needing to be closer to her mother than the chair arrangement permitted. With that adaptation I was able to complete the developmental test in a way that I consider a valid measurement of her present level of development in the sectors measured by the test.

QUANTITATIVE

Developmental age, 58 weeks, 5 days (13.6 months); developmental quotient, 115.

Gross motor: low 56 weeks, high 18 months; average 15 months. Joan walks well, unassisted, on the normal broad base of the toddler. She starts and stops with adequate control for her age. She is able to sit down voluntarily but occasionally falls by collapse when walking. She creeps upstairs on all fours. She is able to climb up onto an adult chair and to pick up a toy from the floor without falling. No abnormal movements are seen.

Fine motor: low 52 weeks, high 15 months; average 13 months (56 weeks).
Joan has good enough arm, hand, and finger control to build a tower of two cubes; she probably could place the pellet in the bottle but this is interfered with by her insistence on eating the pellet and her

refusal, when eating is restricted, to make an effort to insert it. Voluntary release is adequate enough to send the ball with a slight cast toward the examiner. She is able to hold a cup to drink from. She does not do the imitative scribbling with the crayon on the paper. No abnormal movements are seen. Skills are about equal in the two hands. While she is very involved in moving about today, her control and use of her hands are also seen to be very well developed.

Adaptive: 52 weeks, high 15 months; average 13 months (56 weeks).

The peak item is the tower of two at the 15-month level. At the 13-month (56 week) level Joan shows her awareness of the relationship between the round form and the formboard by inserting the round form. She is able to remove and replace a peg in the pegboard. She places a cube into the cup without this having been demonstrated for her. She looks at pictures in the book briefly. She has both the concept of the object out of sight and the motivation and initiative to recover the toy hidden behind the solid screen by making a detour around the screen. (While the following are not test items they suggest something about her understanding: she tries to put the head back on the toy rubber dog when it has fallen off; her mother reports that at home she tries to open cabinets having some awareness of the procedure involved.) She seems to remember where a number of things are kept at home. She does a moderate amount of mouthing of the test materials and her insistence on mouthing the crayon and the pellet interferes to some extent with her test performance with these objects. Her attention is quite focused and her preferences strong and unmistakable.

Language: Low 52 weeks, high 56 weeks; average 54 weeks, 4 days.

Joan vocalizes *dada* in a specific manner, says *baba* for bottle, and has some equivalent of byebye. Mrs. O. reports that Joan says *mama* but connects it with nothing or nobody. She understands such verbal commands from her mother as "Come back here," "Open your mouth," "Show me your teeth." She reacts to her mother's saying "nursery school" with smiling and excitement and her mother feels she understands this as referring to our center. She will give a toy upon request when a gesture is used, will imitate words, has incipient jargon, and obviously recognizes the names of a few objects. Vocalization is sparse in the test situation, a not unusual occurrence.

Personal-social: Low 52 weeks, high 15 months; average 14½ months.

Joan's awareness of people is well developed in terms of recognition and selective interaction. Today she turns to her mother in time of stress but is friendly to me when she feels safe. She studies my face a few times, smiles at me, looks somewhat perplexed when I give her something she does not understand; she glowers and looks angry when crossed. She joins in a simple ball game with me, releasing the ball with a slight cast in my direction. She shows or offers toys, casts objects in play or when she wants to refuse them. She is reported to finger feed herself in part and to indicate her wants by vocalizing.

QUALITATIVE

Appearance: Joan is comfortably dressed in red overalls and striped shirt. She comes into the examining room half pushing, but mainly carrying, a musical push toy. She has an interesting, mobile face and an alert expression. She looks sturdy, healthy, and active. As before, her activity, liveliness, and animation and the interesting changes in facial expression make her an attractive child.

Affect: Joan's expressed feelings include happy chortling, quiet pleasure, a facial expression suggesting puzzlement when given a particular toy. She demonstrates fussing in a slightly anxious way to get to her mother, angry fussing when interfered with, an occasional coy smile, and later when walking about the room a quiet jargon "commentary" accompanying her activity which seemed to suggest a kind of quiet pleasure. There are several episodes of relatively short duration when her mother is trying to get her to stop mouthing the crayon and pellet when her behavior seems deliberately oppositional. This does not persist for long, however.

Activity: Joan's pleasure in physical activity is very apparent. She moves in a well organized way conveying an impression of vigor and great energy. Movements are quite well modulated for a baby of her age. She is able to use activity both to seek something she wants and to avoid something she does not want.

Social Responses: As she has behaved with me for some time, Joan becomes friendly and responsive but is clearly a bit wary in the beginning. She eventually joins me in some little games of mutual imitation such as dotting with the crayon and attempting to imitate stirring with the spoon in the cup, but she is not a great imitator. She plays a ball game with me. She occasionally hands me a toy. She exchanges a few smiles. Her oppositional behavior, which is definite but not terribly strong, is related entirely to her mother. I believe that she is not sufficiently comfortable with me at this time to directly oppose me though she is able to avoid me by moving away, turning away, pushing things off the table, or throwing down things I offer that she does not wish to do.

Striking Features: While Joan remains quite active, her development is smoother and better integrated at this examination than it was at 39 weeks. She performs at an age adequate or better level in all areas with a good balance between the sectors. Language and adaptive behavior, which were lagging behind at the last examination, possibly because of her intense preoccupation with mastering locomotion, are today well developed. She also has more interest in and energy for social interchanges. She appears on the threshold of many areas of new learning as she enters the second year.

Jackie A. Age: 30 mos., 23 days

Jackie was accompanied by both parents for his 30-month evaluation today. He was friendly and in good spirits and quite cooperative with the testing for the most part. In general he much preferred the performance items to the verbal items; he was mildly oppositional a time or two but not in any way that interfered with the validity of the evaluation.

QUANTITATIVE

Developmental age, 40 months; developmental quotient, 129.
Gross Motor: Level 36 months.

Jackie moves easily and gracefully, riding a tricycle well using the pedals, standing on one foot, jumping and landing lightly on both feet, walking up and down stairs alternating feet; he throws and kicks a ball vigorously. His movements are well coordinated and he clearly enjoys physical activity.

Fine Motor: Low 30 months; high 42 months; average, 40½ months.

Jackie is very skillful in the use of his hands; he builds a tower of ten cubes without difficulty, strings the small beads easily and is able to cut the paper manipulating the scissors reasonably well. Other items of eye-hand coordination such as building the three cube structure are performed easily. No abnormal movements are seen.

Adaptive: Low, 30 months; high, 48 months; average, 47 months.

Jackie's performance in this area and in language development reflect his excellent intellectual ability. At the 36-month level, for example, is his ability to imitate the five cube block structure, to name missing parts of the picture, to complete the Seguin formboard and the picture puzzle, to identify geometric forms, and to add three parts to the incomplete man. In the drawing situation he also performs quite adequately at the 36-month level. He matches four primary colors and names three of them reliably. He has the capacity for sustained attention to tasks that interest him. He clearly enjoys many of the tasks and feels quite successful much of the time. He already has high standards for himself, however, and occasionally seems tense when confronted with a difficult task. Even so, he can usually be persuaded to try something that he, at first, refuses.

Language: Low, 30 months; high, 48 months; average, 36 months.

Jackie's speech is well organized a number of months in advance of his chronological age. He has one success each at 42 and 48 months. His performance is solid at the 36-month level in language production and language comprehension. He has no difficulty, for example, in distinguishing the two prepositions *on* and *under*. Speech contains plurals, he speaks clearly in well-articulated complete sentences and with a very expressive, pleasantly inflected voice. He uses speech to ask and to answer questions and to converse. He refuses the comprehension questions today, one of the times when refusal was clearly oppositional, and does not respond to the Action Agents questions. With the latter, it was difficult to tell whether it was a refusal or whether he did not know how to respond.

Personal-social: Low, 36 months; high, 42 months; average 41 months.

Jackie is very competent in self-help skills. For example, he washes and dries his hands and face, puts on his shoes, and manages buttons. He feeds himself well with minimal spilling. He knows his name and sex. He plays cooperatively with other children and speaks of himself and others, relating events of his daily life; he participates in routines, particularly in school but to a certain extent at home as well when given an opportunity. He is a very alert and friendly child who makes a very good contact. There is no doubt that he sees this place and the staff as essentially friendly and trustworthy and is quite responsive to all of us.

QUALITATIVE

Appearance: Jackie remains a very attractive child. This morning he looks generally well nourished and sturdy. He is nicely dressed for the occasion but comes with unwashed hands and unkempt hair, very much in the manner we have seen him on many previous occasions. He is friendly, not anxious, active, and ready to be engaged.

Affect: As indicated above he is for the most part free from anxiety. He does become somewhat tense and anxious at times when asked to do something he is unable to do. He also appears self-conscious a few times, particularly when asked to identify parts of his own body. He is flirtatious and playful in a manner appropriate for a child of his age who is having a good time with an adult. He conveys pleasure by smiling, talking in an animated way, and asking questions. He does not express any active displeasure during this session, but I have seen him do so certainly at other times and know him to be quite capable of being clear and vehement about his displeasure. The range of affective expression of which he is capable is quite wide. He is in good control of his feelings throughout the session and later, I am told, during the physical examination. When asked to wait for something he is usually able to do so without showing great impatience or disappointment.

Activity: There is no sign of inhibition of motor activity nor does Jackie become overactive during the session. Movements are very smoothly coordinated and well modulated. There is every evidence of substantial pleasure in physical activity.

Social response: As indicated elsewhere Jackie responds to the examiner in a friendly way with minimal anxiety. He clearly expects reasonable behavior from me and is able to be reasonable in turn. He is quite involved with the developmental testing situation, and although he looked at his mother occasionally he does not ask for any help from her.

Striking features: Jackie remains quite a remarkable and delightful child. He is very bright, a fact which is an important asset for him. Moreover, his parents value his intelligence. In addition, he is quite a charming and lovable child who even when he is quite needy manages reciprocal relationships with adults, relationships which make them enjoy him and want to take care of him. It seems especially unfortunate for Jackie that the family's contact with us and our involvement in providing substitute care for him ends at this time. While things are very much better than they were earlier, there is no doubt that he is going to continue to have a stressful family situation.

Bibliography

Abelin, E. L. (1975), Some Further Observations and Comments on the Earliest Role of the Father. *International Journal of Psychoanalysis*, 56:293–302.

Ainsworth, M. (1963), The Development of Infant-Mother Interaction among the Ganda. In : *Determinants of Infant Behavior*, vol. 2, ed. B. M. Foss. London: Methuen, pp. 67–112.

——— (1964), Patterns of Attachment Behavior Shown by the Infant in Interaction with His Mother, *Merrill-Palmer Quarterly*, 10:51–58.

——— (1967), *Infancy in Uganda: Infant Care and the Growth of Love.* Baltimore: Johns Hopkins University Press.

——— & Bell, S. M. (1970), Attachment, Exploration, and Separation: Illustrated by the Behavior of One-Year-Olds in a Strange Situation, *Child Development*, 41:1, pp. 49–67.

Aldrich, C. A. (1946), High Lights on the Psychology of Infancy. *Mental Hygiene* 30:590–96.

Alpert, A., Neubauer, P. B., & Weil, A. (1956), Unusual Variations in Drive Endowment. *The Psychoanalytic Study of the Child*, New York: International Universities Press, 11:125–63.

Anders, T. F. (1978), State and Rhythmic Process. *Journal of the American Academy of Child Psychiatry*, 17:401–20.

Anthony, E. J. (1970), The Influence of Maternal Psychosis on Children—Folie À Deux. In: *Parenthood, Its Psychology and Psychopathology*, ed. E. J. Anthony & T. Benedek. Boston: Little, Brown, pp. 571–95.

Barnett, C., Leiderman, P., Grobstein, R., & Klaus, M. (1970), Neonatal Separation. *Pediatrics*, 45:197–205.

Benedek, T. (1959), Parenthood as a Developmental Phase. *Journal of the American Psychoanalytic Association*, 7:389–417.

Benedek, T. (1970), Fatherhood and Providing. In: *Parenthood, Its Psychology and Psychopathology*, ed. E. J. Anthony & T. Benedek. Boston: Little, Brown & Co., pp. 167–83.

Benjamin, J. (1961), The Innate and Experiential in Development. In: *Lectures in Experimental Psychiatry*, ed. H. Brosin. Pittsburgh: University of Pittsburgh Press, pp. 19–42.

———— (1963), Further Comments on Some Developmental Aspects of Anxiety. In: *Counterpoint*, ed. E. Gaskill. New York: International Universities Press, pp. 19–42.

Bergman, P., & Escalona, S. K. (1949), Unusual Sensitivities in Very Young Children. *The Psychoanalytic Study of the Child*. New York: International Universities Press, 3/4:333–52.

Biber, B. (1977), A Developmental-Interaction Approach: Bank Street College of Education. In: *The Preschool in Action*, 2nd ed., ed. M. C. Day & R. K. Parker. Boston: Allyn & Bacon, Inc., pp. 423–60.

———— & Franklin, M. B. (1967), The Relevance of Developmental and Psychodynamic Concepts to the Education of the Pre-School Child. *Journal of the Academy of Child Psychiatry*, 6:5–24.

Bibring, G. L. (1959), Some Considerations of the Psychological Processes in Pregnancy. *The Psychoanalytic Study of the Child*. New York: International Universities Press, 14:113–21.

———— Dwyer, T. F., Huntington, D. S., & Valenstein, A. F. (1961), A Study of the Psychological Processes in Pregnancy and of the Earliest Mother-Child Relationships: I. Some Propositions and Comments. II. Methodological Considerations. *The Psychoanalytic Study of the Child*. New York: International Universities Press, 16:9–72.

Bowlby, J. (1951), *Maternal Care and Mental Health*. Geneva: World Health Organization Monograph no. 2.

———— (1958), The Nature of the Child's Tie to His Mother. *International Journal of Psychoanalysis*, 39:350–73.

———— (1969), *Attachment and Loss*, vol. 1, *Attachment*. New York: Basic Books.

———— (1973), *Attachment and Loss*, vol. 2, *Separation, Anxiety and Anger*. New York: Basic Books.

Brazelton, T. B. (1973), *Neonatal Behavioral Assessment Scale*. London & Philadelphia: Spastics International Medical Publishers.

———— (1974), Does the Neonate Shape His Environment? In: *The Infant at Risk*, ed. S. Bergsma, Birth Defects: Original Article Series, vol. 10, no. 2. New York & London: Intercontinental Medical Book Corp., pp. 131–40.

———— Koslowski, B., & Main, M. (1974), The Origins of Reciprocity. In: *The Effect of the Infant on Its Caregivers*, ed. M. Lewis & L. A. Rosenblum. New York: John Wiley & Sons, pp. 49–76.

———— Young, G., & Bullowa, M. (1971), Inception and Resolution of Early Developmental Pathology: A Case History. *Journal of the American Academy of Child Psychiatry*, 10:124–35.

Bronfenbrenner, U. (1974), Is Early Intervention Effective? In: *A Report on Longitudinal Evaluations of Pre-School Programs*, vol. 2, ed. U. Bronfenbrenner. Washington, D.C.: U.S. Government Printing Office.

Buhler, K. (1929), *Die Krise der Psychologie*. Jena: Fisher.

Coelho, G. V., Hamburg, D. A., & Adams, J. E. (1974), eds. *Coping and Adaptation*. New York: Basic Books.

Cohen, D. J. (1974), Competence and Biology: Methodology in Studies of Infants, Twins, Psychosomatic Disease, and Psychosis. In: *The Child in His Family*: vol. 3, *Children at Psychiatric Risk*, ed. E. J. Anthony & C. Koupernik. New York: John Wiley & Sons, pp. 361–94.

———— Granger, R., Provence, S., & Solnit, A. (1975), Mental Health Services. In: *Issues in the Classification of Children*, vol. 2, gen. ed. Nicholas Hobbs: Washington, D.C., Jossey-Bass Publishers, pp. 88–122.

Coleman, R., Kris, E., & Provence, S. (1953), The Study of Variations of Early Parental Attitudes, *The Psychoanalytic Study of the Child*. New York: International Universities Press, 8:20–47.

Consortium for Longitudinal Studies (1978), *Lasting Effects after Preschool*, Final Report of Department of Health, Education, and Welfare Grant 90-C-1311. Denver: Education Commission of the States.

Cooper, M. (1957), *Pica*. Springfield, Ill.: Charles C. Thomas.

Emde, R. (1980), Toward a Psychoanalytic Theory of Affect: II. Emerging Models of Emotional Development in Infancy. In: *The Course of Life: Psychoanalytic Contributions toward Understanding Personality Development*, vol. 1: *Infancy and Early Childhood*, ed. S. I. Greenspan & G. Pollock. Washington, D.C.: National Institute of Mental Health.

———— Gaensbauer, T. J., & Harmon, R. J. (1976), *Emotional Expression in Infancy: A Biobehavioral Study*. Psychological Issues, A Monograph Series, vol. 10, no. 37. New York: International Universities Press.

Erikson, E. H. (1950), *Childhood and Society*. New York: W. W. Norton.

———— (1953), Growth and Crises of the Healthy Personality. In: *Personality in Nature, Society and Culture*, ed. C. Kluckhohn, H. A. Murray, & D. Schneider. New York: Knopf, pp. 185–225.

———— (1959), *Identity and the Life Cycle*, Psychological Issues, vol. 1, no. 1, monograph 1. New York: International Universities Press.

———— (1964), Human Strength and the Cycle of Generations. In: *Insight and Responsibility: Lectures on the Ethical Implications of Psychoanalytic Insight*. New York: W. W. Norton.

Escalona, S. K. (1962), The Study of Individual Differences and the Problem of State. *Journal of the American Academy of Child Psychiatry*, 1:1, 11–37.

———— (1963), Patterns of Infantile Experience and the Developmental Process. *The Psychoanalytic Study of the Child*. New York: International Universities Press, 18:197–244.

———— (1965), Some Determinants of Individual Differences in Early Ego Development. In: *Transactions of the New York Academy of Sciences*, ser. 2, vol. 27, no. 7, pp. 802–17.

———— (1968), *The Roots of Individuality*. Chicago: Aldine Publishing Co.

Fantz, R. L. (1966), Pattern Discrimination and Selective Attention as Determinants of Perceptual Development from Birth. In: *Perceptual Development in Children*, ed. A. H. Kidd & J. L. Rivoire. New York: International Universities Press, pp. 143–73.

Ferholt, J. B., & Provence, S. (1976), Diagnosis and Treatment of an Infant with Psychophysiological Vomiting. *The Psychoanalytic Study of the Child*, 31:439–59.

Fraiberg, S. (1971), Intervention in Infancy: A Program for Blind Infants. *Journal of the American Academy of Child Psychiatry*, 10:3, pp. 381–405.

———— (1977), *Insights from the Blind*. New York: Basic Books.

———— Smith, M., & Adelson, E. (1969), An Educational Program for Blind Infants. *Journal of Special Education*, 3(2), pp. 121–39.

Freud, A. (1965), *Normality and Pathology in Childhood: Assessments of Development*. New York: International Universities Press, pp. 10–24.

———— & Burlingham, D. (1944), *Infants without Families: The Case for and against Residential Nurseries*. New York: International Universities Press.

Freud, S. (1905), Three Essays on The Theory of Sexuality. *Standard Edition*. London: The Hogarth Press, 7:173–206.

———— (1926), Inhibitions, Symptoms, and Anxiety. *Standard Edition*. London: The Hogarth Press, 20:77–175.

Fries, M. E., & Woolf, P. J. (1953), Some Hypotheses on the Role of the Congenital Activity Type in Personality Development. *The Psychoanalytic Study of the Child*. New York: International Universities Press, 8:48–62.

Furman, E. (1974), *A Child's Parent Dies: Studies in Childhood Bereavement*. New Haven: Yale University Press.

Gesell, A., Amatruda, C., Ames, L. B., Castner, B., Halverson, H., Ilg, F., & Thompson, H. (1940), *The First Five Years of Life: A Guide to the Study of the Preschool Child*. New York: Harper.

Goldfarb, W. (1945), Psychological Privation in Infancy and Subsequent Adjustment. *American Journal of Orthopsychiatry*, 15:247–55.

Goldstein, J., Freud, A., & Solnit, A. J. (1973), *Beyond the Best Interest of the Child*. New York: The Free Press.

Gray, S., & Wandersman, L. (1980), The Methodology of Home-Based Intervention Studies: Problems and Promising Strategies. *Child Development*, 51, 4:993–1009.

Green, M. (1980), The Pediatric Interview and History. In: *Pediatric Diagnosis*, 3rd ed. Philadelphia, London, Toronto: W. B. Saunders Company, pp. 3–5.

———— & Haggerty. R. J. (1977), eds. *Ambulatory Pediatrics*, vol. 2. Philadelphia: W. B. Saunders Company, p. 1.

Greenacre, P. (1959), Play in Relation to Creative Imagination. *The Psychoanalytic Study of the Child*. New York: International Universities Press, 14:61–80.
―――― (1969), Discussion of Dr. Galenson's Paper on The Nature of Thought in Childhood Play. In: *Emotional Growth: Psychoanalytic Studies of the Gifted and a Great Variety of Other Individuals*. New York: International Universities Press, pp. 353–64.
Halverson, H. M. (1937), Studies of the Grasping Responses of Early Infancy. *Genetic Psychology*, 51:371–449.
Harter, S. (1978), Effectance Motivation Reconsidered: Toward a Developmental Model. *Human Development*, 21:34–64.
―――― & Zigler, E. (1974), The Assessment of Effectance Motivation in Normal and Retarded Children. *Developmental Psychology*, 10:169–80.
Hartmann, H. (1939), *Ego Psychology and the Problem of Adaptation*. New York: International Universities Press, 1958.
―――― (1950), Psychoanalysis and Developmental Psychology. *The Psychoanalytic Study of the Child*. New York: International Universities Press, 5:7–17.
―――― (1952), The Mutual Influences in the Development of Ego and Id. *The Psychoanalytic Study of the Child*. New York: International Universities Press, 7:9–30.
Hartmann, H., Kris, E., & Loewenstein, R. (1946), Comments on the Formation of Psychic Structure. *The Psychoanalytic Study of the Child*. New York: International Universities Press, 2:11–38.
Heinicke, C. M., & Strassmann, L. H. (1980), The Effects of Day Care on Pre-schoolers and the Provision of Support Services for Day Care Families. In: *Policy Issues in Day Care: Summaries of Twenty-One Papers*. Washington, D.C.: U.S. Department of Health, Education, and Welfare, Office of the Assistant Secretary for Planning and Evaluation, pp. 87–90.
Jackson, E., & Klatskin, E. (1950), Rooming-In Research Project: Development of Methodology of Parent-Child Relationship Study in a Clinical Setting. *The Psychoanalytic Study of the Child*. New York: International Universities Press, 5:236–74.
Jacobson, E. (1964), *The Self and the Object World*. New York: International Universities Press.
Kagan, J., & Lewis, M. (1965), Studies of Attention in the Human Infant. *Merrill-Palmer Quarterly*, 11:2.
Kennell, J., Gordon, D., & Klaus, M. (1970), The Effect of Early Mother-Infant Separation on Later Maternal Performance. *Pediatric Research*, 4:473–74.
Kessen, W. (1961), Selection and Test Response in Measures in the Study of the Human Newborn. *Child Development* 32:7–24.
Kessen, W. (1965), *The Child*. New York: John Wiley & Sons.

Klaus, M., & Kennell, J. (1976), *Maternal Infant Bonding.* Saint Louis: The C. V. Mosby Company.

Korner, A. F. (1974a), Individual Differences at Birth: Implications for Child Care Practices. In: *The Infant at Risk,* ed. D. Bergsma. New York: Intercontinental Medical Book Corp. Birth Defects: Original Article Series, vol. 10, no. 2, pp. 51–61.

——— (1974b), The Effect of the Infant's State, Level of Arousal, Sex, and Ontogenetic Stage on the Caregiver. In: *The Effect of the Infant on Its Caregiver,* ed. M. Lewis & L. Rosenblum. New York: John Wiley & Sons, pp. 105–21.

——— & Grobstein, R. (1967), Individual Differences at Birth: Implications for the Mother-Infant Relationship and Later Development. *Journal of the American Academy of Child Psychiatry,* 6:676–90.

Kris, E. (1948), On Psychoanalysis and Education. *American Journal of Orthopsychiatry,* 18:622–35. Also in *The Selected Papers of Ernst Kris* (1975). New Haven: Yale University Press, pp. 36–53.

——— (1950), Notes on the Development and on Some Current Problems of Psychoanalytic Child Psychology. *The Psychoanalytic Study of the Child.* New York: International Universities Press, 5:24–46.

——— (1951), Opening Remarks on Psychoanalytic Child Psychology. *The Psychoanalytic Study of the Child.* New York: International Universities Press, 6:9–17.

——— (1975), The Nature of Psychoanalytic Propositions and Their Validation. In: *The Selected Papers of Ernst Kris.* New Haven: Yale University Press, pp. 3–23.

Lamb, M. E. (1976), *The Role of the Father in Child Development.* New York: John Wiley & Sons.

Leiderman, P. H., & Seashore, M. J. (1975), Mother-Infant Neonatal Separation: Some Delayed Consequences. In: *Parent-Infant Interaction,* Ciba Foundation Symposium 33. Amsterdam: ASP (Elsevier Excerpta Medica North Holland), pp. 213–39.

Leonard, M. F. (1971), The Significance of Pica in Children. *Connecticut Medicine,* vol. 35, no. 8:479–82.

Lewis, Melvin (1971), *Clinical Aspects of Child Development,* Philadelphia: Lea & Febiger.

Lewis, Michael (1972), State as an Infant-Environmental Interaction: An Analysis of Mother-Infant Interaction as a Function of Sex. *Merrill-Palmer Quarterly,* 18:95–121.

Lewis, M., & Lee-Painter, S. (1974), An Interactional Approach to the Mother-Infant Dyad. In: *The Effect of the Infant on Its Caregiver,* ed. M. Lewis & L. A. Rosenblum. New York: John Wiley & Sons, pp. 21–48.

Lustman, S. (1956), Rudiments of the Ego. *The Psychoanalytic Study of the Child.* New York: International Universities Press, 11:89–98.

Mahler, M. (1966), Notes on the Development of Basic Moods: The Depressive Affect. In: *Psychoanalysis, a General Psychology: Essays in Honor of Heinz Hartmann*, ed. R. M. Loewenstein, L. M. Newman, M. Schur, & A. J. Solnit. New York: International Universities Press, pp. 152–68.

——— Pine, F., & Bergmann, A. (1975), *The Psychological Birth of the Human Infant*. New York: Basic Books.

Mechanic, D. (1974), Social Structure and Personal Adaptation: Some Neglected Dimensions. In: *Coping and Adaptation*, ed. G. V. Coelho, D. Hamburg, & J. E. Adams. New York: Basic Books, pp. 32–44.

Millikan, F. K., Layman, E. M., Lourie, R. S., & Takahashi, L. Y. (1968), Study of an Oral Fixation: Pica. *Journal of the American Academy of Child Psychiatry*, 7:79–107.

Murphy, L. B. (1972), Infants' Play and Cognitive Development. In: *Play and Development*, ed. M. W. Piers. New York: W. W. Norton, pp. 119–26.

Murphy, L. B. (1974), Coping, Vulnerability and Resilience in Childhood. In: *Coping and Adaptation*, ed. G. V. Coelho, D. A. Hamburg, & J. E. Adams. New York: Basic Books, pp. 69–100.

Naylor, A. K. (1970), Some Determinants of Parent-Infant Relationships. In: *What We Can Learn From Infants*, ed. L. Dittman. Washington, D.C.: National Association for the Education of Young Children, pp. 25–47.

Nunberg, H. (1932), *Principles of Psychoanalysis: Their Application to the Neuroses*. New York: International Universities Press, 1955.

Pavenstedt, E., ed. (1967), *The Drifters*. Boston: Little, Brown & Co.

Peiper, A. (1949), *Cerebral Function in Infancy and Childhood*. Translation of the 3rd revised German edition. Nagler & Nagler, New York Consultants Bureau, 1963.

Piaget, J. (1951), *Play, Dreams, and Imitation in Childhood*. New York: W. W. Norton.

——— (1952) *The Origins of Intelligence in Children*. New York: International Universities Press.

——— & Inhelder, B. (1969), *The Psychology of the Child*. New York: Basic Books.

Powers, G. F. (1949), Remarks to Undergraduate Students of Clinical Medicine. In: *Modern Perspectives in Child Development* (1963), ed. A. J. Solnit & S. Provence. New York: International Universities Press, pp. 3–9.

Provence, S. (1965), Disturbed Personality Development in Infancy: A Comparison of Two Inadequately Nurtured Infants. *Merrill-Palmer Quarterly*, 11:2:149–70.

——— (1966), Some Aspects of Early Ego Development: Data from a Longitudinal Study. In: *Psychoanalysis, a General Psychology: Essays in Honor of Heinz Hartmann*, ed. R. M. Loewenstein, L. M. Newman, M.

Schur, & A. J. Solnit. New York: International Universities Press, pp. 107–22.

———— (1972), Psychoanalysis and the Treatment of Psychological Disorders of Infancy. In: *Handbook of Child Psychoanalysis*, ed. B. B. Wolman. New York: Van Nostrand Reinhold Co., pp. 191–220.

———— (1974), Some Relationships between Activity and Vulnerability in the Early Years. In: *The Child in His Family*, vol. 3, *Children at Psychiatric Risk*. New York: John Wiley & Sons, pp. 157–66.

———— (1977), Some Clinical Applications of Research on Parent-Child Relationships. In: *Child Psychiatry: Treatment and Research*, ed. M. McMillan & S. Henao. New York: Brunner/Mazel, pp. 207–21.

———— (1978), Application of Psychoanalytic Principles to Treatment and Prevention in Infancy. In: *Child Analysis and Therapy*, ed. J. Glenn. New York: Jason Aronson, Inc., pp. 581–96.

———— & Lipton, R. (1962), *Infants in Institutions*. New York: International Universities Press.

———— Naylor, A., & Patterson, J. (1977), *The Challenge of Daycare*. New Haven: Yale University Press.

———— & Ritvo, S. (1961), Effects of Deprivation on Institutionalized Infants: Disturbances in Development of Relationship to Inanimate Objects. *The Psychoanalytic Study of the Child*. New York: International Universities Press, 16:189–205.

Rapaport, D. (1959), A Historical Survey of Psychoanalytic Ego Psychology. In: *Identity and the Life Cycle*, Psychological Issues, by E. H. Erikson. New York: International Universities Press, vol. 1, no. 1, monograph 1, pp. 5–17.

Rescorla, L., Provence, S., & Naylor, A. (1982), The Yale Child Welfare Research Program: Description and Results. In: *Day Care*, ed. E. Zigler & E. Gordon. Boston: Auburn House Publishing Co., pp. 183–99.

Richmond, J. B., & Lipton, E. L. (1961), Studies on Mental Health of Children with Specific Implications for Pediatricians. In: *Prevention of Mental Disorders in Children*, ed. G. Caplan. New York: Basic Books, pp. 95–121.

Richmond, J., & Lustman, S. (1955), Autonomic Function in the Neonate: Implications for Psychoanalytic Theory. *Psychosomatic Medicine*, 17:269–75.

Sander, L. (1962), Issues in Early Mother-Infant Interaction. *Journal of the Academy of Child Psychiatry*, 1:141–66.

———— (1964), Adaptive Relationships in Early Mother-Child Interaction. *Journal of the Academy of Child Psychiatry*, 3:2, pp. 231–64.

———— (1969), Regulation and Organization in the Early Infant Caretaker System. In: *Brain and Early Behavior*, ed. R. J. Robinson. New York & London: Academic Press.

———— (1970), Early Mother-Infant Interaction and Twenty-four Hour

Patterns of Activity and Sleep. *Journal of the American Academy of Child Psychiatry*, 9:103–23.

———— (1975), Infant and Caretaking Environment: Investigation and Conceptualization of Adaptive Behavior in a System of Increasing Complexity. In: *Explorations in Child Psychiatry*, ed. E. J. Anthony. New York: Plenum Press, pp. 129–66.

———— (1980), Investigation of the Infant and Its Caregiving Environment as a Biological System. In: *The Course of Life: Psychoanalytic Contributions Toward Understanding Personality Development*, vol. 1: *Infancy and Early Childhood*, ed. S. I. Greenspan & G. H. Pollock. Washington, D.C.: National Institute of Mental Health, 177–201.

Schilder, P. (1935), *The Image and Appearance of the Human Body*. New York: International Universities Press, 1950.

Seashore, M., Leifer, A., Barnett, C., & Leiderman, P. (1973), The Effects of Denial of Mother-Infant Interaction on Maternal Self-Confidence. *Journal of Personality and Social Psychology*, 26:369–78.

Senn, M. J. E. (1948), The Psychotherapeutic Role of the Pediatrician. *Pediatrics*, 2:147–53.

———— & Green, M. (1958), Teaching of Comprehensive Pediatrics on an Inpatient Hospital Service. *Pediatrics*, 21:476–90.

———— & Solnit, A. J. (1968), *Problems in Child Behavior and Development*. Philadelphia: Lea & Febiger.

Shapiro, E., & Biber, B. (1972), The Education of Young Children: A Developmental Interaction Approach. *Teachers College Record*, 74:1, pp. 55–79.

Spitz, R. (1945), Hospitalism: An Inquiry into the Genesis of Psychiatric Conditions in Early Childhood. *The Psychoanalytic Study of the Child*. New York: International Universities Press, 1:53–74.

———— (1946), Hospitalism: A Follow-up Report. *The Psychoanalytic Study of the Child*. New York: International Universities Press, 2:113–17.

———— (1950), Relevancy of Direct Infant Observation. *The Psychoanalytic Study of the Child*. New York: International Universities Press, 5:66–73.

———— (1965), *The First Year of Life: A Psychoanalytic Study of Normal and Deviant Development of Object Relations*. New York: International Universities Press.

———— & Wolf, K. (1946), Anaclitic Depression: An Inquiry into the Genesis of Psychiatric Conditions in Early Childhood, vol. 2. *The Psychoanalytic Study of the Child*. New York: International Universities Press, 2:313–42.

Stechler, G., & Latz, E. (1966), Some Observations on Attention and Arousal in the Human Infant. *Journal of the Academy of Child Psychiatry*, 5:517–25.

Stern, D. N. (1971), A Micro-Analysis of Mother-Infant Interaction: Behavior Regulating Social Behavior Between a Mother & Her 3½-Month-

Old Twins. *Journal of the American Academy of Child Psychiatry*, 10:501–17.

———— (1974), Mother and Infant at Play: The Dyadic Interaction Involving Facial, Vocal and Gaze Behavior. In: *The Effect of the Infant on Its Caregiver*, ed. M. Lewis & L. Rosenblum. New York: John Wiley & Sons, pp. 187–213.

Thomas, A., Chess, S., & Birch, H. G. (1968), *Temperament and Behavior Disorders in Children*. New York: New York University Press.

Trickett, P., Apfel, N., Rosenbaum, L., & Zigler, E. (1982), A Five-Year Follow-up of Participants in the Yale Child Welfare Research Program. In *Day Care*, ed. E. Zigler & E. Gordon. Boston: Auburn House Publishing Co., pp. 200–22.

Waelder, R. (1932), The Psychoanalytic Theory of Play. *Psychoanalytic Quarterly*, 2:208–24.

Wallerstein, J., & Kelly, J. (1975), The Effects of Parental Divorce: The Experience of the Preschool Child. *Journal of the American Academy of Child Psychiatry*, 14:4, pp. 600–16.

———— (1980), *Surviving the Breakup*. New York: Basic Books.

White, R. W. (1959), Motivation Reconsidered: The Concept of Competence. *Psychological Review*, 66:297–333.

White, B. (1975), Critical Influences in the Origins of Competence. *Merrill-Palmer Quarterly*, 21:243–66.

Winnicott, D. (1960), The Theory of the Parent-Infant Relationship. *International Journal of Psychoanalysis*, 41:585–95.

Wolf, K. (1948), Unpublished Seminar Notes.

Wolff, P. H. (1966), The Causes, Controls and Organization of Behavior in the Neonate. *Psychological Issues*, 5:17.

Yarrow, L. J. (1964), Separation from Parents during Early Childhood. In: *Review of Child Development Research*, ed. M. L. Hoffman & L. W. Hoffman. New York: Russell Sage Foundation, pp. 89–136.

———— (1981), Beyond Cognition: The Development of Mastery Motivation: In: *Zero to Three: Bulletin of the National Center for Clinical Infant Programs*, ed. S. Provence. Washington, D.C., 1:3, pp. 1–5.

———— & Pederson, F. A. (1976), The Interplay between Cognition and Motivation in Infancy. In: *Origins of Intelligence*, ed. M. Lewis. New York: Plenum Press, pp. 379–99.

———— Rubenstein, J. L., & Pederson, F. A. (1975), *Infant and Environment: Early Cognitive and Motivational Development*. New York: John Wiley & Sons, Halsted Division.

Zigler, E., & Gordon, E., eds. (1982), *Day Care: Scientific and Social Policy Issues*. Boston: Auburn House Publishing Co.

Index

Action research, 6, 58, 59–60
Adams, J. E., 152
Adaptation, 6, 27, 29, 30, 52–58; components of successful, 152; mutual, 40, 44, 52–53; in parenthood, 38, 150–51, 152–56
Affectionate behavior (examples), 185–86
Aggressive behavior, 38, 48
Ainsworth, M., 42n
Alpert, A., 28
Anders, T. F., 28
Anxiety, 36, 50
Apfel, N., 7, 144–45, 146–47, 154
Attachment behavior, 42–43n
Attachment theory, 42–43n
Attachments (friendships), 143
Autonomous ego functions, 28, 42

Bank Street College of Education, 56
Behavior, 29–30, 36
Bell, S. M., 43n
Benedek, T., 37
Bergmann, A., 41
Biber, B., 56
Bibring, G. L., 37, 38
Birch, H. G., 28, 29
Body, development of postural model of, 106
Bowlby, J., 42n
Brazelton, T. B., 28, 44
Brazelton Scale, 11
Bronfenbrenner, U., 150
Bühler, Karl, 50

Caregiver(s), 15, 33, 39–40; continuity in, 15, 17, 41, 42. *See also* Fathers; Mothers; Parents
Caring, 164
Chess, S., 28, 29
Child care: parental attitudes and, 32; phase concept and, 37; in Yale program, 3, 10, 15–17
Child care counseling (Yale program), 22, 56; use of, analyzed, 142
Child development information, abstract, 142
Clinical practice: intervention and, 58–59; model of, 25; modification of 20–21
Coelho, G. V., 152
Cognitive development, 6, 15, 53, 55, 56
Cohen, D. J., 29, 157
Coleman, R., 38
Competence, 52, 53
Compliance, 119–20
Conflict: among toddlers (examples), 183–84
Congenital characteristics. *See* Endowment
Continuity: of competent personnel, 158; of daycare, 162; of health care, 12, 48, 159; of primary caregiver, 15, 17, 41, 42; of staff/parent relationship, 4, 46
Coping, 14–15, 52–58, 152, 154
Culture, 40

Daycare: developmental, 162–63; as essential service, 157, 162–64, 164; experience considerations in, 34–35; incidents (with comment), 169–86; observation categories for, 193

211